There is Another Way

*Guidance and hope for the dissatisfied
and the disillusioned*

Philip McParland

D0765957

Soul Space

A Soul Space Publication

Copyright © Philip McParland 2015

ISBN 978-1-63452-720-0

A catalogue record of this book is available
from the British Library

Cover image © Nemeziya/Shutterstock.com

Cover design by Joshua Horgan, Oxford

Typeset and printed by Joshua Horgan, Oxford

For the memory of my Mum and Dad

There are some people I wish to thank for their
help in the production of this book.

To Carmel and Liz for their encouragement
to write. To Gerry, Maureen, Rose, Daniel,
Kathleen, Liam and Flo for their honest
and constructive feedback. To Josepha and Dave
for the use of their apartment in my native
Co. Armagh in Northern Ireland.
And finally to the members of my family for
their interest and support.
I am most grateful to you all.

There is Another Way

*Guidance and hope for the dissatisfied
and the disillusioned*

Contents

A Parable

There is a Sufi parable about the human condition. A Sufi master had lost the key to his house and was looking for it in the grass outside. He got down on his hands and knees and started running his fingers through every blade of grass. Along came a number of his disciples. They said, "Master, what is wrong?"

He said, "I have lost the key to my house."

They said, "Can we help you find it?"

He said, "I'd be delighted."

So they all got down on their hands and knees and started running their fingers through the grass.

As the sun grew hotter, one of the more intelligent disciples said, "Master, have you any idea where you might have lost the key?"

The Master replied, "Of course. I lost it in the house."

"Why then are we looking for it out here?" they all exclaimed.

"Isn't it obvious?" said the Master. "There is more light here."

Introduction

Writing a book for public reading is something I never saw myself doing. It wasn't on my list of projects. But such is the conviction I have about the human condition that I had to write, to put my thoughts down on paper. Conviction is not conviction if it does not come from personal experience. This little book has certainly been inspired by my own journey, especially that part of my journey which began in my late forties. But it has also been inspired by the work I do with people. I am a spiritual counsellor and facilitator. I meet with people for one to one accompaniment and I facilitate small group workshops. Most people I spend time with come to me because they experience some kind of dissatisfaction and want their lives to be different. They may not be clear about what this difference means but they know something needs to change.

There are a number of ways of naming the change that people are looking for. For those in a mid life transition the change is a change from the first half of life to the second half of life. For those with a religious faith the change can be named as a movement from the institutional stage of religion to the mystical stage of religion. For everyone the change involves letting go of one lifestyle and finding another. Sooner or later we come to admit that the lifestyle we are used to is not working for us and we go looking for an alternative, for another way. This is what happened to me. The way I was living was leaving me dissatisfied and disillusioned; something needed to change in my life. This book is an attempt to share my experience. It is written with those who are ready for a new lifestyle in mind; to offer them some guidance and hope. I say ready because unless we are ready no change is likely to take place. Desire for change is not enough. We need to be in the right place in ourselves if it is to happen.

As the sub title suggests this book is aimed at those who are experiencing dissatisfaction and disillusionment in their lives. While people at most ages and stages can experience some form of dissatisfaction and disillusionment there are some groups who are particularly susceptible to it. These are those in the mid life transition, those who have been made redundant and those recently retired. In my view what these groups experience makes them more open and ready to find another way. If you are in one of these groups I hope this little book may offer you some timely help. I am of course aware that my approach may not be suited to everyone who finds themselves adrift and struggling. This is because the book makes explicit reference to God, scripture and prayer. It draws inspiration from the life and teaching of Jesus and it proposes some spiritual practices. It is my personal view that spirituality has an important role in helping us create a different lifestyle. But the spirituality that runs through this book is not the spirituality of one particular church. It is a Christian spirituality that is inclusive. It is a spirituality that those who belong to any church as well as those who do not attend church can find relevant, meaningful and hopefully accessible.

I have discovered that there is one thing that needs to happen if people are to experience the change they are looking for. This is the acceptance of unconditional love. If we are not willing or able to accept the fact that we are loved unconditionally then it will be very difficult if not impossible for us to live another way. Accepting unconditional love is in fact not easy. As wounded human beings we have all kinds of resistance to it. Much of the work I do with people centres on helping them accept that they are loved and lovable as they are. I find that people need guidance and support if they are to 'claim their belovedness' as I like to call it. For this reason you will notice that the acceptance of unconditional love is a theme that runs throughout this book. It will be there explicitly, but more often implicitly. By the end I hope you will be convinced that the acceptance of unconditional love is the thing that makes all the difference.

I have tried to make the book both inspirational and practical. The first part attempts to describe and analyse the lifestyle driven by what I call the A triangle. This lifestyle is very familiar to us. It seems to be one we simply fall into, especially in the first half of life when we are under the influence of the false self. It is certainly rife in what we refer to as the 'developed world.' This is why I call part one 'The Default Way.' The second part puts forward an alternative lifestyle. This lifestyle is the other way referred to in the book's title. It is built around three values all beginning with the letter C. It is a lifestyle that can bring us true happiness and deep fulfilment. The third part offers an overview of the journey of life and seeks to explain what needs to happen to us and in us if we are to move from one lifestyle to another. Because change is often very difficult this process can take some time. Furthermore, it may not be as linear as my overview suggests. Part three is a kind of map of the journey of life. Having a map of the landscape helps us to know where we are, even though we may not always take the most direct route! Finally, at the end, as an appendix, I have a chapter for those women and men who live religiously dedicated lives known as religious life. It is my belief and I am speaking from some experience that many of them are feeling the need for a new lifestyle.

I believe this book can help you grow in the kind of self knowledge that allows you to see and accept that there may be a difference between what you long for and what you settle for. The material I present and the way I present it is not meant to be a judgement on you and your life. It is simply offered to help you understand yourself, the way you may be living and the way you are in fact meant to experience your life. This is the reason why at the end of each chapter I offer some questions for personal reflection. If you are able and willing to spend some time with these questions I am confident you will find the exercise beneficial and rewarding. I have also included a list of relevant books at the end for those who may wish to do some further reading and reflecting. This is a self help book, hence the invitation to do a bit of work!

Finally, a few words about myself. For over thirty years I was a member of a religious order. During this time I was involved in Church ministry at all levels and in a variety of ways. I was chaplain and teacher in a secondary school, I worked in retreat centres in Ireland, England and Scotland, I served in a parish, I edited a religious magazine, I accompanied students in their formation and I was director of vocations. By the time I got to fifty I was tired and disillusioned. In mid life I had reached a crisis point in my life. My mid life transition brought to a head all the things in me that I had been avoiding during the first half of my life in the hope that they would simply go away, which of course didn't happen. It was a time of struggle, confusion, anxiety and at times loneliness and desolation. With help I was able to work through my 'issues.' This process led me to make the decision to leave religious life and to create a new lifestyle and ministry. I am now trying to practice the lifestyle I describe in part two of this book. I am also offering a ministry that seeks to help others move into this lifestyle. Even though I have written this book in an objective way, it is in fact much of my own story and journey. There are times when this is obvious. When it may not seem obvious my own experience is still the main source of inspiration. I hope this will make what I have to say more credible.

Part 1
The Default Way

"What I want to do, I don't do. And what I don't want to do I find myself doing."
Paul of Tarsus

"Here we are with an unbounded desire for happiness and not the slightest idea of where to look for it."
Thomas Keating

Chapter 1
The A Triangle

"So many people seem to be looking for happiness in the wrong place."

This is what I hear many people say about the way they experience themselves and their lives:

- *I never quite feel good enough*
- *I am exhausted trying to be perfect*
- *I feel I have to be busy*
- *I worry too much about what other people think of me*
- *I am continually pushing myself*
- *My life is driven by expectations*
- *I am overly concerned about the way I look*
- *I need to feel useful and productive*
- *I am measuring myself by what I do*
- *I spend too much money on things I do not need*
- *I have lost trust in institutions*

There is no doubting the fact that many people today are dissatisfied. They are driven by unrealistic expectations. They do not feel good about themselves. They have to keep themselves busy, but are not sure what it is that is making them restless. What is the real cause of all this dissatisfaction? Why are so many people experiencing themselves as inadequate and worthless? I would like to suggest that the main culprit is what I call the **A Triangle**. The A triangle is a powerful driving force at work in our western culture. First world culture is driven by three A's – Accumulation, Achievement and Approval. By these things we determine the success of our lives. By these things we define who we are. By these things we measure our self worth. The A Triangle is our default programme for happiness. It is rife in our society. It drives our capitalist and consumerist lifestyle. It operates in all our institutions. It even plays a role in the way our churches function and make decisions.

The A Triangle powerfully and often subtly has us believe that we are what we have, we are what we do, and we are what other people think of us. In other words our value is external; it comes from and is dependent on things outside ourselves. If my value comes from accumulation, achievement and approval, from what I have, from what I do and from what other people think of me, then I will never feel good about myself. What is more I will never be happy because I will never be satisfied with who I am and with my life.

Powerful Voices

It is no surprise that Jesus was offered the A Triangle at a significant time in his life. Before he began his public ministry around the age of thirty he spent some time on his own in preparation. The scriptures tell us that he went into the desert. There, as he looked into his heart, he found three powerful voices tempting him. These voices can be expressed like this. Build your life around possessions (accumulation). Build your life around power (achievement). Build your life around performance (approval). To each of these voices Jesus said 'no.' I am not what I have. I am not what I do. I am not what other people think of me. Jesus ability to say 'no' to these voices gave him the freedom to begin his mission to practice and preach the Kingdom. Indeed the success of his ministry depended on his willingness not to define himself by external sources of value. Jesus knew that his value came from the relationship which he had with the One he called Abba, Father. Jesus had an internal source of value.

False Identity
When I present the A Triangle to people, especially people who are reflective, I usually get a very positive response. They recognise almost immediately that it is present not just in our culture but also in their own lives. Perhaps this is the key; to see how the A Triangle is present and at work in ourselves. Because of what happened to us in childhood we each took on our own external source of value and a false identity. A

good description of this false identity is offered by Marcus Borg, an American theologian and writer.

"All of us already have an identity, though it may be difficult to name it concisely. We acquire a sense of who we are from our socialization and our ongoing life, from the relationships and forces that shaped and continue to shape us. These include relationships with family and friends, the effects of school and work and perhaps Church, and also the impact of the wider culture in which we live. Culture has a powerful effect on us. Our culture bombards us with messages that shape our sense of who we are and what is worth valuing. In the United States, the central values of our culture are the "three A's": attractiveness, achievement, and affluence. For many of us, our sense of who we are depends upon how well we measure up to these identity-conferring values that operate in our psyches, as well as to the other messages we have received about who we are and what we should do.

Thus, no matter how good our parenting was, we grow up wounded. Our socialization and life in culture confer conflicting and conflicted identities. Not only are we not whole, but many of us have a low, sometimes desperately low, sense of self-worth. As a result, all of us need the formation of a new identity."(1)

Because of the three A's we each need the formation of a new identity. The formation of this new identity takes time and a degree of personal work. The A triangle is deeply imbedded in us and its power is very strong. Thankfully it is possible to break it but we need to be ready and willing to enter into a process of change and growth that we may not find easy.

Wrong Places

The A triangle keeps us living at a superficial level with no real depth to our lives. We need to move beyond questions like: How do I look? How did I do? How much money am I going to make? In the A triangle there is no interiority, no intimacy and no real involvement. And interiority, intimacy and involvement are where we need to get to. We need a connection with our own inner world of longing and desire, deep communication with at least one other person, and contact with those who need help and support.

Returning to the parable at the beginning, many of us have lost the key to our house. In our search we look for it in the apparent light of the A triangle. Even though we know that the key is to be found inside the house we look for it outside. The house of course represents happiness. The human condition has us look for happiness in the wrong places, in things that can never satisfy us. It makes us search desperately for happiness where it cannot be found. Happiness can only be found inside. The key is not in the grass; it was not lost outside ourselves. It was lost inside ourselves. This is where we need to look for it.

Medical Evidence

Recent medical evidence published in England is very revealing and relevant to what I am suggesting. In 2013 there were 1,000 million prescription drugs dispensed in England alone, an increase of 350 million from 2003. This means that nearly 50% of the population are currently taking prescription drugs costing the National Health Service in excess of £15 billion per year. The three most common sets of drugs prescribed are for the treatment of high blood pressure, cholesterol and depression. Accepting the fact that there may be some over treating and unnecessary prescribing this quite shocking information from a fairly typical western European country suggests that something is having an adverse effect on our physical and emotional health. Many professionals believe this is our lifestyle and they say more needs to be done to help people change their style of life. It is my view that the lifestyle they are referring to is the A triangle. The restless search for happiness in accumulation, achievement and approval is making us physically and emotionally unwell. I invite you to check this out for yourself. What are the main things that are causing stress in your life? Where is the pressure you experience coming from? Why do you sometimes find yourself feeling exhausted and dissatisfied? Perhaps what I write about in the next three chapters will help you find some answers.

In a Nutshell

Many people find themselves stressed and dissatisfied. The cause of this stress and dissatisfaction is accumulation, achievement and approval – the A triangle. The A triangle has us look for happiness in things outside us, in what we have, in what we do and in what other people think of us. The A triangle can never make us happy because it is an external source of value.

Questions for personal reflection

I suggest that you spend some time with these questions and perhaps do some journaling with them.

1. How do you react to the idea of the A triangle?
2. Do you agree that the A triangle is rife in our western culture? In what ways do you see it at work?
3. Which of the three A's do you think is most dominant in your life?

4. Do you accept the view that our contemporary western lifestyle is the major cause of physical and emotional ill health? Is it affecting your physical and emotional health? How do you feel about this?

Chapter 2
Accumulation

It is not the man who has too little,
but the man who craves more, that is poor.
Seneca, Epistulae Morales

Let us be honest. The dominant philosophies in the so called first world are capitalism and consumerism, making money and spending money. Western economies are driven by these philosophies. Our economies have become so dependent on banks that when the financial crisis happened in 2008 governments almost immediately bailed them out with huge sums of money. It was as if governments could not take the risk of even asking the question: Is there another way for our economy to function? Without hesitation we returned to the very things that failed us: capitalism and consumerism.

In the 21st century we have a whole new set of cathedrals. These give expression to a new form of worship! They are our shopping centres and malls. They are the places where many of us spend our free time, including our Sundays which traditionally have been about rest and religious worship. It seems we cannot get enough things and have enough possessions. The credit card makes sure of this!

Prosperity

A number of years ago I heard the prime minister of a European country describe the success of his term of office as greater prosperity for his people. If the main priority of a government is to create wealth for its people then surely it is measuring people's worth by what they have, by their possessions. I lived in Ireland during some of what is referred to as the Celtic Tiger years. The country was awash with money. People were spending as if there was no tomorrow. Because very few seemed to be willing to say, 'I have enough' many got badly caught when the bubble burst. The Irish experience suggests that even a country with a long and rich spiritual tradition can succumb to greed and accumulation.

I am not denying that we need material possessions. Of course we do. What I am suggesting is that in a culture which puts so much emphasis on material possessions we can end up defining ourselves by what we have. The implications of this are many. The more we have the better we may feel about ourselves. Owning a big house and a big car, both status symbols, will make us feel important, even significant. The more we have the more secure we will feel. Surely the underlying emotional dynamic at work here suggests that we are what we have and we are what we own. To measure ourselves and others by possessions and ownership is superficial. It creates a false sense of identity and ultimately leads to emptiness and even depression.

Retail Therapy

Accumulation is very attractive, very powerful and very subtle. Notice how you can feel after a day's shopping? Words like satisfied, comforted, contented, come to mind. No wonder we now use the expression 'retail therapy' to describe the effect shopping may have on us. Buying things has a feel good factor. Whether we use or wear many of the things we buy doesn't seem to matter. What seems to be more important is emotional effect the experience has on us. No wonder there is a lot of waste! The truth is, if we need to be constantly buying in order to feel good about ourselves then surely our value comes from what we have, not from who we are. Associating personal value with accumulation is dangerous, not least because a time will come when we will have to let go of our possessions.

We cannot take our material possessions with us when we die. They will be no good to us in the presence of God. Even though we know this, it still does not prevent us from wanting more and more. Why? Yes, we may like to gratify our material needs. Yes, we may like to make life easy for ourselves. Yes, we may like to let others know that we are rich and prosperous. But it is my belief that the real reason has to do with the way accumulation makes us feel about ourselves. If shopping makes us feel good about ourselves we are going to keep doing it. We will keep doing it until we find another source of value, an internal source of value. We will continue to do it until we discover that our self esteem does not depend on it.

Enough

I know a retired business man who lives in Ireland. He told me that about two years before the collapse of the economic boom known as the Celtic Tiger he said to himself, 'I do not need to make by business any bigger. I do not need to take any more risks. I am content with what I have. I have enough.' He said that it was this decision to accept that he had enough which saved his business when the down turn came and which ensured that he had some financial security in his retirement.

Nowadays it seems many of us cannot get enough. We cannot get enough of goods, of information, of food, of work, of options. We make and we spend; we produce and we consume. What is all this consumption about? What are we hoping it will do for us? Make us happy. Keep us satisfied. Yet the truth is, the more we get the more we want. The Alcoholics Anonymous programme puts it well, "We always need more and more of what does not work." Consumption will never make us happy. It will never fill the hole we have inside us. Perhaps this is what it is really about; filling the emptiness we experience inside. Accumulation cannot fill our inner emptiness. It cannot change the way we feel about ourselves. Only love can do this, especially the greatest love of all which in the words of the Whitney Huston song is the love inside of us. Through accumulation we are looking to external things to make us happy. Things outside of us no matter how many we have will never make us happy because happiness can only be found within.

Entitlement

Accumulation is also partly responsible for the culture of entitlement which is rife in our society. We certainly are living in a culture of entitlement. We have a tendency to convince ourselves that we deserve more and more. And if we do not get what we think we deserve we feel badly treated. In many of our young people entitlement has almost become a way of life. They must have the latest in fashion and technology especially if their peers have the latest. The culture of entitlement also creates the victim mentality. If we do not get what we believe we deserve we feel hard done by, victims. For some people victimhood can become a way of life which in fact is often a way of getting control. Whether overtly or subtlety accumulation is always saying I deserve more. It can lead to a lack of gratitude and an inability to say 'thanks.'

Our Natural Resources

It is also worth mentioning here the effect our insatiable desire to consume has on our planet earth. We are exploiting our natural resources to an alarming degree. Our consumption is impacting the climate which has disastrous consequences, especially on the poorer regions of the world. It is affecting our wildlife whose natural habitats are being destroyed. And of course it is unfair on future generations who deserve a decent quality of life too. We should never forget that we are indebted to those who have gone before us for what we have today. So what are we in our turn going to leave for our children and our children's children? If we continue to consume the way we are there will be little left for those who succeed us.

It is obvious that accumulation is rife in the developed world. It is also obvious that our need to accumulate is fed by the capitalist and consumerist philosophies that drive our economies. What may not be so obvious is the fact that our need to accumulate comes from an emptiness within ourselves which we are reluctant to acknowledge and accept. This emptiness cannot be filled by things no matter how many things we possess.

In a Nutshell

Accumulation is driven by capitalist and consumerist philosophies, by making money and spending money. It is a false attempt to fill the emptiness we experience inside. It prevents us from saying, 'I have enough.' Accumulation has us find our value in what we have, in our possessions.

Questions for personal reflection

Once again I suggest that you spend some time with these questions and perhaps do some journaling with them.

1. Do you think you are accumulating more than you need? If you are, what is the real reason you are doing this?
2. How much influence does advertising have on your shopping habits?
3. How do you react to the story of the business man who said to himself, 'I have enough?' Have you ever said to yourself, 'I have enough?'
4. Have you any concerns about the impact that accumulation is having on global issues?

Chapter 3
Achievement

"We tend to overwork as a means of self-escape,
as a way of trying to justify our existence."
Josef Pieper

A utilitarian philosophy dominates Anglo Saxon culture. In utilitarian philosophy value is equated with usefulness. Only useful activity is valuable, meaningful, moral. Activity that is not clearly, concretely useful to oneself or to others is worthless, meaningless, immoral. Back in the first half of the 19th century Jeremy Bentham and John Stuart Mill identified happiness with utility, pleasure with profit. Their ideas took root and by 1871 an English logician and political economist William Stanley Jevons summed up their philosophy with the words: "Value depends entirely upon utility." It seems to me that this is a thesis that dominates much of western culture today: what is important is usefulness, the profit I can extract from an experience or a possession.

Reflect on your own experience. Have you noticed how the first question we are often asked in social company is not "Who are you?" but "What do you do?" Have you noticed the number of people who seem to feel guilty if they have nothing to 'do?' Have you noticed how many young coronary patients are restless during convalescence and feel guilty when they should relax? Have you noticed how some people feel the need to justify a holiday? It will help us work better when we get back. I have certainly noticed these things. More personally I have noticed some of them operating in my own life. For many years utilitarianism seemed to be in my blood flowing through my body. I had a deep need to be useful and productive which was not only feeding me; it was also driving me. I know from experience the powerful emotional force that is achievement.

Work

Recently an English man I had on retreat told me he believed with conviction that the dominant value in UK culture is work. Work comes first. It is more important than anything else. If this is true, and there is plenty of evidence to suggest that it is, then people are measured by their productivity and by their usefulness. Of course we need to work, but we do not need to define ourselves by our work. If we define ourselves by our capacity for work we lose touch with what it really means to be human. We are, after all, called human beings not human doers!

The consequences of a culture that makes work the number one priority are many. Words like busyness, ambition, competition, exhaustion, burn- out, depression naturally come to mind. But there are other things too, perhaps less obvious. Those who are unemployed or unemployable feel worthless. Those who stay at home to look after children feel devalued. Those who take time to relax and play feel guilty. The work ethic that drives western culture and that supposedly creates prosperity does not make people feel any happier about themselves; in fact it often makes them feel worse.

Busyness

Today many people like to be able to say, "I am busy." What is more, they love to be described by others as 'busy.' It is as if busyness has become some kind of yardstick for measuring personal worth. Busyness is certainly an expression of a contemporary restlessness which may come from deep feelings of insecurity. But busyness is also in part caused by our obsessive need to be productive and useful. If we need to keep ourselves busy the chances are we only feel good about ourselves when we are doing something, especially when we are doing something that is useful. The root cause of busyness is our tendency to measure ourselves by what we do.

Our need to be continually doing something is graphically summed up in this comic strip. The scene is a mother inside the house looking out a window, her little boy sitting in the yard with his back to a tree. This is the conversation between them:

Mother: "Ditto, what are you doing out there?"
Ditto: "Nothing."
Mother: "You must be doing something! Now tell me!"
Ditto: "I'm not doing anything."
Mother: Ditto! You tell me what you're doing!"
Ditto (to himself): "Good gosh!" (He tosses a stone.)
(out loud): "I'm throwing rocks!"
Mother: "I thought it was something like that. Now stop it at once!"
Ditto: "Okay."
(to himself): "Nobody will let you just do nothing anymore."

Needless to say Ditto is most of us. Other people will not let us do nothing. What is more we will not allow ourselves to do nothing. The expectation to achieve not only comes from outside us. It also comes from within us. The pressure to constantly achieve is immense.

Religion
Religion does not help to relieve us of the pressure to achieve and be productive. In fact it can put even more pressure on us. A number of years ago I was giving a day retreat to a parish community in the south of England. As I spoke I noticed a

woman knitting while she listened to me. In the discussion that followed my input she admitted that her conscience would not allow her to do nothing even on a day retreat. She simply could not be wasting time. After all she had been taught that "the devil makes work for idle hands!" This was ironic for at least two reasons. One, the theme of my talk was God's unconditional love. Two, the woman belonged to the tradition within Christianity which originally protested that the Roman Catholic Church was putting too much emphasis on merit. The fathers of the Reformation insisted that we are saved by faith, not by works!

"Look busy! Jesus is coming," is a saying that may bring a smile to our faces. But it does give expression to a belief that is very common in the lives of Christian people of all churches. Many Christians believe that Jesus expects them to be busy and productive. Their Jesus is a demanding Jesus and in order to win his approval and favour they feel they have to be constantly doing something. They are afraid that Jesus will 'catch' them idle!

Nowadays it is not uncommon to hear people say that they are spiritual but not religious. There is no doubting the fact that a gap has developed between religion and spirituality. This is unfortunate. Religion needs spirituality and spirituality needs religion. Perhaps one of the reasons why people have become disillusioned with religion is because it tends to make them feel unworthy and guilty. It sends out a message that God's love needs to be earned, that we need to do something or be someone in order to win God's approval and favour. Spirituality on the other hand encourages us to take possession of the relationship which God has with us and to let ourselves be loved by this God as we are. It puts love before rules and regulations, relationships before achievement.

Jesus insisted that the Father's love is gift, not achievement. In his Father's vineyard those who started work in the late afternoon received the same wage as those who began in the early morning. The Father does not measure us according to our productivity and performance. In the religion of Jesus who we are is much more important than what we do. If our religion is making us feel guilty because we are not productive enough or busy enough then it is not the religion of Jesus.

Power
Our tendency to find our value in what we do also creates the desire for power and its consequences – ambition and jealousy. Power can be motivated by our need to be in control which in turn makes us feel secure; the more power we have the more secure we think we will feel. But being in a position of power can also make us feel significant. If I need to be in a position of power in order to feel

important then once again I am finding my value in what I do, not in who I am. The significance that comes from being 'powerful' is making me feel good about myself. There is a saying that power corrupts and absolute power corrupts absolutely. There is no doubting that power has a corrupting effect on people. This will happen if it is feeding our own needs rather than serving the needs of others. When power is motivated by self interest it can be destructive. If it is power that is making me feel worthwhile then I will never have enough of it! It is with good reason that the great teacher, Jesus, understood where the desire for power in the human heart comes from and instead recommended a spirituality of powerlessness and service.

In childhood most of us were encouraged to be productive, to achieve many things, even great things. Achievement is of course necessary. Without it there would be no human and scientific progress and development. But there is a great danger in putting too much emphasis on achievement. We end up measuring ourselves by what we do rather than by who we are. The evidence suggests that far too many people living in the developed world are doing this. If we idolise achievement then, like Jeremy Bentham, we make usefulness the purpose of human life and we rob our lives of the things that give us delight and pleasure.

In a Nutshell

Achievement is rife in Anglo Saxon culture. It is influenced by a utilitarian philosophy which equates value with usefulness. It finds expression in the contemporary obsession with busyness, with productivity, with success. It also contaminates our religious experience; we need to earn God's love by our efforts and good deeds. Achievement has us find our value in what we do.

Questions for personal reflection

Once again I suggest that you spend some time with these questions and perhaps do some journaling with them.

1. Do you agree that a utilitarian philosophy dominates Anglo Saxon Culture?
2. Are you someone who tends to spend too much time working? If so, what is the real reason for this?
3. Do you feel guilty when you have nothing to do? Where is this guilt coming from?
4. Are you a busy person? If so, why?
5. If you are a religious person, does your religion make you feel that you need to earn God's love by your achievements? Would you like a religion that frees you from the expectation to achieve?

Chapter 4
Approval

*"A man cannot be comfortable
without his own approval."*
Mark Twain

Our need for approval is very strong. What other people think of us matters a great deal. How we are perceived by others has an effect on the way we feel about ourselves. We have a tendency to allow the opinions other people have of us to define who we are. There are many examples of this in our contemporary culture. Here are some, perhaps the more obvious ones.

Physical Appearance

Our bodies are important and we need to take care of them. Good diet, regular exercise and sufficient sleep contribute to a healthy body, which in turn helps our mental health. Respect for our bodies is essential if we are to live well and feel well. Of course respect for our bodies also includes taking an interest in our physical appearance. When we take an interest in our physical appearance we are happier with ourselves and we are happier in the company of other people.

However, I believe it is fair to say that there is an over preoccupation, if not obsession, with physical appearance nowadays. It is a fact that huge amounts of money are spent every day on every kind of cosmetic. The cosmetic industry is a multi-billion pound business. Television advertising seeks to convince us that money spent on beautifying our bodies is money well spent, because "we are worth it!" Recently I heard a woman say that the cosmetics industry is built on the poor self esteem of women.

What are the implications of this preoccupation with physical beauty known as the cult of the body beautiful? One is that we tend to idolise those who are beautiful. Hollywood and the movie industry make sure of this. Another implication is that we may judge people by the way they look. We think that what is on the outside is more important than what is on the inside. And then most importantly of all we may judge ourselves by the way we look. Our self esteem is determined by our appearance. This latter implication is a huge issue, one, I believe, of major concern. The entertainment industry, the fashion industry and the cosmetics industry all make us believe that if we are attractive we will be accepted by others and if we are accepted by others we will feel good about ourselves. The underlying message here is that our value comes from our physical appearance, from the way we look. But we cannot allow our value to be dependent on something that changes and eventually fades. The fact is beauty is only skin deep. Physical beauty cannot last no matter how much money we spend on it.

Social Image

We have an expression, "Keeping up with the Joneses." It suggests that our social standing is important to us. We like to be seen as having as much as our friends and neighbours. Perhaps our desire to keep up with the Joneses also indicates that we do not want others to be better than us. The days of making distinctions between people on the basis of class may be over but status still seems to matter. If we create the perception of success and wealth we will be looked up to and considered important by the people around us. And what other people think of us affects how we see ourselves.

Perhaps a good contemporary example of social image is the type of car we drive. Cars seem to be a public statement. Perhaps they are a statement of personal significance. Perhaps they are a way of letting everyone know that we have made something of ourselves. Something tells me that they may in fact be a way of seeking approval. If they are intended to draw attention, to get notice, they certainly work. But do we really need the latest and best model of our favourite car in order to feel significant and win the approval of others? Surely significance and approval has to be based on something much less superficial. The appearance of status does not necessarily make us feel any better about ourselves. In fact, it can mask feelings of inadequacy and low self esteem.

Social Media

A contemporary phenomenon is the rapid development and widespread use of social media. Those who use the social media say that it is about connection. Of course we have a need for connection, but what kind of connection is the social media promoting? Why do some of us need to let our Facebook 'friends' know what we are having for our evening meal or what we are wearing on a night out? Perhaps the honest thing to say is that we are seeking their approval. The success of our Facebook page seems to be determined by the number of 'likes' we have. The term 'like us on Facebook' used to advertise this form of media surely says it all. The approval we may seek through social media carries dangers. The information we put out there can be hijacked and used to exploit us in all sorts of ways, including sexual exploitation. There is a cost if we seek approval in the wrong ways and in the wrong places.

Politics

Approval also seems to be a major driving force in the world of politics. Politicians are concerned about their approval ratings. Whether they admit it or not they like to know how they are doing in the polls and this indication of performance is important to them. Because of their need for approval, political leaders often do the popular thing rather than the right thing. Politicians need to keep reminding themselves that politics is about good policies not popularity. Of course winning approval is a temptation for all those in leadership whether or not they are elected democratically. Interestingly, Jesus who was a great leader never sought the approval of others for the decisions that he needed to make. If Jesus had been controlled by what other people thought of him he would not have chosen the path of love which ultimately led to his death on the cross.

Performance
Of course it is not just politicians who are preoccupied with winning approval. Actors, musicians, comedians, pop stars, models, celebrities are greatly dependent on the approval of their fans. Indeed it could be said that their profession is an approval profession. When they are performing they are pleasing their supporters. Performance may win them admiration, but without performance they may have no source of approval and when they have no source of approval they may have no sense of personal value and worth. Surely the premature and often tragic

44

deaths of many high profile entertainers bear witness to this reality.

In singling out those in the entertainment industry there is the danger we will think that they are the only ones addicted to performance. The truth is most of us hope to get approval from our performance. This is something we picked up in early childhood when we needed to measure up to the expectations and demands of our parents and other significant adults. Sadly, as I mentioned earlier, it is also something that influences many people's relationship with God. To win God's approval and God's favour we are convinced that we need to put in a good performance. A performance model of life and a performance model of religion are rife and it is not that easy to let go of either of them.

In whatever way it expresses itself our need for approval is yet another external source value. Once again we are looking for something outside ourselves to make us feel good about ourselves inside. But we cannot get our value from what other people think of us. No matter how much approval we get from other people it will never be enough to satisfy us. We will still be left looking for more and more. If we are to learn to be ourselves then we need to stop seeking the approval of others. Let me conclude this chapter with the same quotation I offered at the beginning. "A man cannot be comfortable without his own approval." These are the words of Mark Twain who seemed to have such a wonderful insight into human nature. They are clear about where we need to get to. It certainly took me time and effort to get there. But it has been worth the struggle! I had to find my own approval, and to stop seeking the approval of others.

In a Nutshell

Our need for the approval of others is very powerful and very pervasive. It takes many forms of expression some subtle, some not so subtle. These can range from the way we look to the type of car we drive to how we use the social media. Politics can also be driven by a desire for approval; so can our need to put in a good performance. Approval has us find our value in what other people think of us.

Questions for personal reflection

Once again I suggest that you spend some time with these questions and perhaps do some journaling with them.

1. Is approval something that you are constantly looking for? What are the ways in which you seek approval?
2. Are you overly preoccupied with your appearance? If so, why? Are you concerned about your social image? If so, why?

3. What is the real reason you need the approval and recognition of others?
4. Inspired by the words of Mark Twain, what do you need to do to find your own approval?

Chapter 5
The True Self and the False Self

"Anyone who wants to save his life must lose it. Anyone who loses his life will find it. What gain is there if you win the whole world and lose your very self? What can you offer in exchange for your one life?"
Matthew 16:25-26

The terms 'true self' and 'false self' have become familiar to us to recent times. This is probably because of the way psychological insights have been popularised and made accessible. Spirituality nowadays also frequently refers to the true self and the false self as realities that impact on our spiritual growth and development. In order to properly understand the underlying causes of the A triangle and why it has such control over us we need to understand what we mean by the true self and the false self.

The true self is the self created by God. It is our fundamental identity, our core truth, who we are in the eyes of God. The true self knows that it is loved as it is, unconditionally. It also knows that it is unique and gifted. Unfortunately very early in life we became disconnected from our true self. At some point in childhood we did not get the love we needed from our parents. The pain of this was too much for us to cope with at that very young age. The true self became wounded and was unable to remain true to itself. Sooner or later two things happened: (1) the true self went into hiding in order to protect itself; (2) another self developed around the demands and expectations of parents. This other self was an acquired self, an idealised self, a false self.

Parents want a child that they will find easier to love, a child that will fit in with their needs and their requirements. The child then becomes the kind of person its parents want it to be. The child becomes the person its parents want it to be, rather than the person it needs to be (its true self). It does this because it cannot survive without the love and affirmation of its parents. The child's identity is then formed around a false self and this false self becomes its default mode of living.

A Personal Example

To illustrate this let me offer an example from my own life. My father was a perfectionist. His expectations of me and my six siblings were very high. He wanted me to be the best. There was nothing wrong with this in itself. The problem however was that my father's affirmation and praise were given or withheld on the basis of whether or not I lived up to his standards. Because

I needed his affirmation and praise I strove to be the kind of person he wanted me to be. Anything less than perfect was a failure making me feel that I was neither loved nor lovable. Understandably I also became a perfectionist because I needed to be perfect to feel worthy of love. For years I was unable to accept and love myself as I am, imperfect and flawed.

The Wound of Conditional Love

The false self is created by the childhood wound of conditional love. Because the false self is built around conditional love it needs us to do something or be something in order to feel good about itself. The false self has an external source of value. It needs to find its value in things outside itself. This makes it turn to the three A's for its identity and happiness. In fact, the false self and the three A's feed off each other. Indeed, like the hen and the egg it is not possible to say which comes first. There is certainly no doubting the fact that the more we build our lives around accumulation, achievement and approval the more embedded in us the false self becomes and therefore the more difficult it is to let go of its power and control.

It is often said that change begins within. Change is essentially an inside job. This is certainly true when it comes to breaking the power of accumulation, achievement and approval. The best chance we have of letting go of our emotional dependency on the three A's is by facing up to our false selves. We need to name and accept the way the false self is at work within us. What is more, we need to surrender the control it has over us. The truth is, at some stage in adult life the power of the false self needs to be broken and the true self needs to re-emerge and be nurtured. This involves a process that can be difficult and emotionally painful. It is the process that I will describe in section three when I offer some thoughts on the mid life transition. First I want to talk about an alternative way to find happiness. I prefer to present the vision first. I believe that if we know there is an alternative way to live that offers us delight in ourselves, joy in relationships and fulfilment in serving others we are more likely to embrace the process I refer to in section three.

In a Nutshell

The A triangle feeds our false selves and prevent us from experiencing our true selves. In order to break the emotional control the A triangle has over us we need to claim our true selves and tame our false selves.

Questions for personal reflection

Once again I suggest that you spend some time with these questions and perhaps do some journaling with them.

1. Have you heard of the terms 'true self' and 'false self' before? Do they make sense to you?
2. What kind of person do you need to be in order to feel worthy of love?
3. Are you ready to face up to the way the false self is operating in your life?

Part 2
Another Way

*"I shall be telling this with a sigh
Somewhere ages and ages hence:
Two roads diverged in a wood, and I –
I took the one less travelled by,
And that has made all the difference."*
Robert Frost

*"First there is the fall, and then we recover
from the fall. Both are the mercy of God."*
Julian of Norwich

Chapter 6
The Three Circles

"It was a new sense of release and assurance and peace with myself and a genuine interest in other people that I hadn't experienced before."
Jimmy Carter

If the false self creates and colludes with the A triangle what is it that can help us access and develop the true self? I would like to suggest that we claim and nurture the true self by practicing three values which I call the three C's. These values are contemplation, companionship and compassion. Unlike the three A's which naturally fit into a triangular shape the three C's are three concentric circles with contemplation in the centre circle, companionship in the second circle and compassion in the outer circle. The idea of the three C's being circular suggests that they are inclusive and heart-centred values. The three C's were practiced and preached by Jesus. They are what Jesus meant by belonging to the Kingdom of God. They put relationships at the centre of our lives.

A few years ago I took some time to look at the way the false self had been operating in my life. I came to a point in the process where I knew I had to find something to replace it, something meaningful and life-giving, otherwise the A triangle would pull me back into its seductive world. During one of my daily walks the idea of the three C's came to me. At that moment I had an insight that I knew in my head and in my heart was right. It provided me with a way forward for my life. Since then I have tried to build my life around the values of contemplation, companionship and compassion. I have also sought to promote these values in the work that I do. Needless to say practicing and promoting the three C's has not been straight forward. I have had both successes and failures. But my commitment to them gives me meaning, fulfilment and hope.

Contemplation is a real experience of God's love. It is to know in our hearts that we are loved unconditionally, as we are. It enables us to claim our original blessing, our belovedness, and therefore to realize that the love we need is in fact inside of us. Contemplation is experienced through forms of prayer that help us to receive, to listen, to be, to let ourselves be loved, to accept the gift that has already been given to us.

Companionship is the experience of unconditional acceptance, of mutual listening, of soulful conversation, of enjoying a shared meal. It satisfies the longing in the human man heart for connection and intimacy. It is one of the most beautiful gifts we can give to each other.

Compassion is reaching out to others, especially those who are struggling. It does not make distinctions between people, nor does it judge by appearances. Compassion offers us a way to become involved in the lives of other people and to build an inclusive community in the world.

Firm Foundations

There is a solid basis for the three C's. They have firm foundations in Christian theology. Unfortunately and sadly in the way Christianity is lived these theological foundations can be neglected and ignored. Too often Christianity is experienced as a meritocracy where everything has to be achieved and earned. The Gospel is not a requirements religion. And because the three C's are Gospel values they have nothing to do with requirements. Instead they have everything to do with gift. The justification for the three C's is to be found in who God is and in what God freely offers us. For this reason they are the house built on the rock that Jesus refers to in one of his parables (Matthew 7:24-25). Hopefully the following brief summary of the three main theological foundations of the three C's will help to convince you that there is no need to associate the religion of Jesus with fear and guilt. Hopefully too it might help to relieve you of any pressure you feel because of the expectations and demands you may have internalised.

Love is unconditional. God's love for us is free, unmerited, gratuitous, pure gift. The Christian life is not about winning God's approval or God's favour. It is not about making ourselves acceptable to God. We do not need to earn God's love. Our efforts, our good deeds do not make God love us. God's approval, God's favour, God's love, is given. It is a fact. God cannot not love us unconditionally because God is unconditional love. From the moment we were conceived we were loved unconditionally and unconditional love will have the last word. This is the only real biblical promise.

The primacy of being over doing. Our value is intrinsic; it comes from within, from the belovedness we were born with. We are human beings, not human doers. Who we are is more important than what we do. I once heard God compared to a mother who took her three young children to the seaside on a summer's day. The children spent most of their time on the beach playing in the sand. Each of them built a sand castle, according to his or her ability. When they had finished their work their mother came to look at what they had done. She praised each of them individually for their achievements. On returning home the mother fed her children, washed them and put them to bed. Then she sat down to relax. She was pleased with the day at the seaside; pleased that her children enjoyed themselves on the beach and that they were safe; pleased too with the way she encouraged each of them. And in the meantime the tide came in and washed away the sand castles her children had built.

This story is a lovely example of the primacy of being over doing. Who we are matters much more to God than what we do. In God's world being certainly comes before doing.

The spiritual life is God's work in us. Often the practice of religion suggests that we ourselves are solely responsible for our salvation and for our spiritual growth and development. The truth is we are not. We do not save ourselves. We are not meant to save ourselves. In fact, we cannot save ourselves. Jesus is our saviour. He came among us to do for us what we cannot do for ourselves, no matter how hard we try. Similarly, we do not sanctify ourselves. We are not meant to sanctify ourselves. Indeed, we cannot sanctify ourselves. The Holy Spirit is our sanctifier. The Holy Spirit is the one who brings to birth in us the redemption achieved by Jesus. Our salvation and our sanctification are both ultimately God's responsibility. Redemption is God's work in us. On our journey to God, we are meant to take the lift rather than climb the stairs!

Radical Grace

The foundations of the three C's can be summed up in a word that is familiar to most people: Grace.

In Christian theology grace is the word that refers to the free and unmerited favour of God towards us. What we receive from God is always pure gift, given without conditions and requirements. Unfortunately because of pride, the 'original sin,' we have a tendency to forget and even ignore this. Some find it difficult to receive freely. Others prefer to be self sufficient and manage their lives on their own. Many live as if they can 'save' themselves by their own power and strength. No wonder that grace, indeed radical grace, has been the recurring message down through the centuries of the people we describe as mystics. It is also with good reason that during those times when the Christian churches became too smug and proud God sent people, often unlikely people, to remind us that all is grace.

It is because of radical grace that our value is intrinsic, it comes from within. It is because of radical grace that we are loved and lovable as we are. It is because of radical grace that we can say, "We are unconditional love." It is because of radical grace that we have no need to feed our false selves through accumulation, achievement and approval. It is because of radical grace that we can build our lives around the values of contemplation, companionship and compassion. The practice of the values of contemplation, companionship and compassion allows us to experience what radical grace really means.

In a Nutshell

There is a way to claim and nurture our true selves. It is a spiritual path built around the three gospel values of contemplation, companionship and compassion. These three values have their foundation in radical grace.

Questions for personal reflection

Once again I suggest that you spend some time with these questions and perhaps do some journaling with them.

1. What is your initial response to the three C's as an alternative lifestyle?
2. Is it helpful for you to know that the three C's were central to the life and teaching of Jesus?
3. Does the story about the mother who spent the day at the beach with her three children have anything to say to you about the way you may be living your life?

Chapter 7
Contemplation

And did you get what
You wanted from this life, even so?
I did.
And what did you want?
To call myself beloved, to feel myself,
Beloved on the earth.
Late Fragment, Raymond Carver

When Jesus left his home in Nazareth around the age of thirty to begin his public ministry he first made contact with his cousin John who was baptising along the banks of the river Jordan. During the short time they spent together Jesus asked John to baptise him. As Jesus came up from the water he heard a voice saying to him, "You are my Beloved Son in whom I am well pleased" (Mark 1:11). This was the voice of God, his Father, confirming him in his identity. At that moment Jesus knew that he was loved unconditionally by his Father and that his Father took delight in him. It was an experience of contemplation, an experience which, significantly, preceded Jesus' ministry but which prepared him to practice and preach the Kingdom. At the Jordan Jesus knew that his Father's love was gift, not achievement.

Our Belovedness

Contemplation is the experience of love as gift. It is affective knowledge of God's personal love for each of us. We are the Father's children and Abba is pleased with us. Contemplation allows us to experience our belovedness which is our original blessing, the face we had before we were born, as the Buddhists would say. In contemplation our true selves are revealed and we are able to claim our core truth. Through contemplation we realise that our value comes from within, not from anything outside ourselves. In the experience of contemplation we know that everything we need is right here, right now and that this is the place where we are accepted, cherished and safe. In a word, contemplation is to know God as Father.

Because contemplation helps us to find our value within it serves to break the power of the false self which as I have already mentioned has external sources of value. To know ourselves as loved and lovable as we are means that we do not have to look to accumulation, achievement and approval to feed our emotional needs, including the emptiness we experience inside. Contemplation, more than anything else, helps us to claim our true selves and to tame our false selves.

To experience contemplation we therefore need to find practical ways of letting ourselves be loved as we are. There are two in particular that I have found helpful and that I would like to say something about; one is silent prayer; the other is play.

Silence

Today noise is a fact of life. It even has become a way of life. Non-stop television and radio, the constant sound of traffic, music systems, mobile phones all create a level of activity and noise that is impossible to get away from. It is not uncommon to meet students who study with music playing in the background. Indeed some would even admit to the fact that they cannot study without background music. We have become so used to sound in our homes, in our places of work and on our streets that when it is not there we may feel ill at ease. Without noise there is a feeling that something is missing.

Then there are those internal resistances to silence. Silence can make us feel uncomfortable. It can even threaten us. In silence we cannot not listen to what is going on inside us, and we may not want to hear what our hearts are saying to us. In fact, we may be frightened of what is going on in our inner world of thoughts and feelings and desires. If we do not like ourselves we will probably not like silence.

A number of years ago I took an early morning walk through the streets of Dublin. It was summer. The sun was shining brightly, the birds were singing and there was stillness in the air. As

I enjoyed this unusual experience of city silence a young man rode past me on a bicycle. He had a radio tied to his handlebars and it filled the silence with loud pop music. Later I shared my experience with someone I considered wise. His response was perceptive. "Most people prefer to fill silence with noise rather than turn it into solitude." Because of our resistance to silence we seem to prefer noise and if noise is not readily available we will create it. Yet silence offers us an opportunity to experience something very deep and very personal. The late John O'Donohue said that silence, "is one of the most precious things in the human spirit... It can be a homecoming to our own deepest belonging." Our deepest belonging is to God. When we are willing to turn silence into solitude we come to know what it really means to come home to God.

Contemplation is about turning silence into solitude. To experience contemplation therefore we have to actively and deliberately create times of silence in our lives. The discipline of creating times of silence involves two things: a sacred place and a sacred time.

A Sacred Place

A sacred place is a place apart, a place free from distraction and from noise. A sacred place can be anywhere because God is everywhere. It can be in a corner of your bedroom or your living room. It can be in your conservatory or in your attic. The important thing is that it is accessible and easy to get to. In your sacred place you need a chair that is firm but comfortable. It is also good to have a symbol or symbols of the presence of God. These may be a lighted candle or an open bible or a picture or an icon. A sacred place is your place. It is your place to be alone. A sacred place is important because the right kind of environment and atmosphere are important if we are going to spend time in silent prayer.

A Sacred Time

Just as important as a sacred place is a sacred time. A sacred time is a time in the day that you are able to put aside for prayer. The time you chose is one that suits your lifestyle, your circumstances, even your metabolism. Praying after exercise or a big meal is not a good idea! Neither is praying late at night especially if you are a morning person. The time you chose also needs to be one that you can be faithful to with consistency. Changing the time from day to day usually results in prayer being pushed to one side. There will always be more important things to do! The amount of time you should spend in silence is also a very personal thing. It will depend on your commitments and your responsibilities. Some people can give fifteen minutes others can give up to an hour. If you are a beginner it is best to start with ten minutes and then gradually extend this to whatever time your daily schedule can afford. A sacred time is a lifestyle decision that requires discipline. This discipline is worth the effort.

Methods

Once we create times of silence in our daily lives we need to decide what we are going to do in the silence. In other words we need to choose a method of prayer also referred to as a way of praying. To open ourselves to the experience of contemplation it is important that we use the right methods of prayer. Because contemplation is the experience of unconditional love the methods of prayer that we use need to be ones that allow us to listen, to receive, to be, to let ourselves be loved. Using these kinds of methods may be more difficult than we think. We can feel unworthy in the presence of God, undeserving of God's love. We can also fall into the habit of talking to God, even talking non-stop! We may of course need to share our lives with God. But talking can in fact be a way of staying in control of the relationship. Contemplation is about handing control of the relationship over to God and allowing God do what God does best: love us!

A Sacred Image

So let me be practical and suggest a few contemplative ways of praying that you may find helpful. The first involves the use of a sacred image.

It is the Father/Son detail from Rembrandt's well known painting, 'The Return of the Prodigal.'

Sit on a chair that is comfortable, but firm.
Place Rembrandt's meditation image in front of you, perhaps on a coffee table.
Light a candle near the image.
Relax your body and try to let go of what is on your mind.
Spend a few moments looking at the image. Imagine that you are the one being held in the Father's arms. When you are ready hear the Father whisper some or all of these words into your ear:

You are my beloved son/daughter.
I am pleased with you.
I rejoice in you.
I take delight in you.
My love for you is gift.
It has nothing to do with your achievements.
Do not worry about feeling unworthy.
Do not worry about your failures.
You belong to me.
I cherish you.
I love you as you are.
You are safe in my arms.
Allow your heart to come home.

If one of these phrases feels a favourite you might like to stay with it, repeating it slowly. As you repeat the phrase become aware of how it is making you feel. Name the feeling. Own the feeling. Let the feeling express what is happening in your relationship with God.

When you are ready conclude your time of prayer by thanking God the Father for loving you the way He does. Ask Him to continue to protect and care for you in your daily life.

A Mantra

Another contemplative way of praying involves the use of what is known as a mantra. A mantra is a single phrase or word that you repeat over and over until it sinks deep into your heart. Many people have their own personal mantra which they have either chosen for themselves or which was given to them from within. Because I am focusing here on the need to let ourselves be loved as we are I want to suggest mantras that are more suited to this. Here are some to choose from. They are all to be found in the scriptures.

- *"You are precious in my eyes and I love you."*
- *"I have loved you with an everlasting love."*
- *"I have made my home within you"*
- *"You are my beloved daughter/son in whom I am well pleased."*
- *"I have called you by your name and you are mine."*

These mantras are the words of God speaking personally and directly to each one of us. They are words that God wants us to hear and to take to heart.

A good way to do this is to sit in silence with your eyes closed. Relax your body and try to let go of the things that are on your mind. Begin to say the words of the mantra you have chosen. Say them slowly. Repeat them over. As you do, sooner or later you will start to feel their affect. This may bring you to a place of inner silence where you find yourself resting in love without the use of words. This can be a real experience of contemplation. If distractions come, and they usually do, it may be helpful to return to your mantra. Using a mantra in this way can lead to an affective knowledge of God's love. It is an affective knowledge of God's love that allows us to claim our original blessing, our belovedness, which is who we are in the eyes of God.

Imaginative Contemplation
A third contemplative way of praying is one that is actually referred to as an imaginative contemplation. This is one that comes from the Ignatian tradition and is particularly suited to those who have good imaginations. You can do an imaginative contemplation with many passages of scripture. However, if you want your time of prayer to be an experience of love then you need to choose suitable passages. One such passage is the account of the washing of the feet which took

place at the Last Supper. This account is to be found in St John's Gospel chapter 13, verses: 1-13.

Read the passage a couple of times then close your eyes and try to picture the scene in your mind. Imagine the upper room where the Last Supper took place. Sense the atmosphere. See the people who were present; Jesus, the disciples. Put yourself at the table. Notice what this feels like. Now observe Jesus getting up from the table, removing his outer garment, taking a jug of water and a basin in his hands and starting to wash the feet of his disciples. Sense the shock on the faces of the disciples, especially the strong reaction of Peter. Become aware of how you feel as Jesus makes his way to you. Experience Jesus washing your feet; the look on his face as he seeks your approval; the gentle way he pours the water over your feet; the feel of his hands as he wipes the water with a towel; the tenderness with which he kisses the tops of your feet. Allow the experience to affirm you, comfort you, heal you of your feelings of unworthiness and shame. Remember this is Jesus washing your feet, doing something for you and to you that servants do. This is Jesus' way of telling you that you are precious in his eyes and that he loves you. It is his way of showing you that he is a very good friend who is always at your service.

Conclude by having a conversation with Jesus about this very personal encounter you have just had with him. Share with him your feelings. Thank him for his affirmation and tenderness. Ask him to help you serve others in the way that he has served you.

If we want to experience the fruits of contemplation then we must be willing to spend time, daily time if possible, in silent prayer. Making a commitment to silent prayer requires discipline. In this discipline a sacred place, a sacred time and the right kind of method are necessary.

Play

The second thing that I have found helpful in allowing us experience contemplation is play. I realise that for many people play may seem an unusual activity to be associated with contemplation. At first sight it appears to have nothing to do with spirituality. However, I have come to see that play is not just a necessary way of keeping us healthy and balanced. It is also a deep expression of what is most fundamental in our relationship with God. Homo Ludens, man at play, is, in fact, man accepting that the world is God's responsibility and that God loves unconditionally.

Before I offer reasons why I believe play is an experience of contemplation I would like to explain what I mean by play. By play I mean all activity that is free of the obligation to produce and achieve results. In other words activity that does not need any justification and that, therefore, allows a person to be and to rejoice in the act of being.

In play the activity is engaged in for its own sake. The focus therefore is on acceptance and receptivity. By setting aside time, productive time, useful time, to play we are actually acknowledging that life itself is a gift, a gift that comes to us freely and unmerited. The source of this gift is God. Play allows God to love us in the unconditional way God wants to love us. It helps us to accept the gratuity of God's love which is what contemplation it about.

Delight

In his book, *In Tune with the World: A Theory of Festivity*, the German philosopher Josef Pieper recalls a time when he was in Bengal during the great autumn festivals. Struck by the wonderful spirit of joy which permeated these celebrations despite the poverty of the people, Pieper enquired as to the reason for this joy. The answer of one orthodox Hindu ran: *It is the joy of being a creature whom God has created out of joy.* (2) God has created us out of joy, not out of necessity. This means that God takes delight in us because we are and as we are. It also means, by implication, that we can take delight in ourselves because we are and as we are. Play is an expression of this delight. Playful activity is activity that is both non-productive and joyful. It allows us the freedom to be and to rejoice in ourselves. Consequently play helps to affirm what is fundamental to human existence, namely, that our true value as human beings is intrinsic. Our real worth precedes and is independent of achievement, class, role, wealth, fame or any other label which we are tempted to cling to for significance and security. This is what we call our true selves or our belovedness. If play helps us experience our true selves then it is a contemplative activity.

Perhaps in our busy, productive world we have lost the art of play. Many of us do not make enough time for play. We see it as a waste of time, something just for children. We can also feel guilty playing. But, *"What is this life if, full of care, we have no time to stand and stare?"* Play is not a waste of time and it is certainly not something we should feel guilty about. Giving into guilty feelings only keeps us in the world of the A triangle and the false self. We need to give ourselves permission to play. By giving ourselves permission to play we start to experience ourselves in a new way. We come to realize that our value is intrinsic, that it comes from who we are not from what we do. We also gradually come to accept that we are in fact loved unconditionally. To feel comfortable spending time in play is a sign that we are comfortable letting ourselves be loved as we are. And to feel comfortable letting ourselves be loved as we are is a good description of the experience contemplation.

Love's Table

I end this chapter with a poem. It is a poem called 'Love' written by the Welsh born English Poet George Herbert. In the poem Herbert describes God as Love. Love comes to us as gift but we pull back; we feel we don't deserve to be loved in this way. But Love refuses to give up; Love continues to pursue us with a gentle and patient persistence. Love's persistence eventually softens our resistance and we surrender. We sit down at Love's table and taste Love's meat. To surrender to Love, to sit down at Love's table and taste Love's meat is to experience contemplation.

Love bade me welcome: yet my soul drew back,
     Guilty of dust and sin.
But quick-eyed Love, observing me grow slack
     From my first entrance in,
Drew nearer to me, sweetly questioning
     If I lacked anything.

"A guest," I answered, "worthy to be here":
     Love said, "You shall be he."
"I, the unkind, ungrateful? Ah, my dear,
     I cannot look on thee."
Love took my hand, and smiling did reply,
     "Who made the eyes but I?"

75

"Truth, Lord; but I have marred them; let my shame
　　Go where it doth deserve."
"And know you not," says Love, "who bore the blame?"
　　"My dear, then I will serve."
"You must sit down," says Love, "and taste my meat."
　　So I did sit and eat.

In a Nutshell

Contemplation is the experience of our belovedness. It is to know in our hearts that we are loved and cherished as we are, unconditionally. Two things in particular can help us experience contemplation. These are silent prayer and play.

Questions for personal reflection

Once again I suggest that you spend some time with these questions and perhaps do some journaling with them.

1. What are the things that prevent you from spending some time in silence?
2. Try one of the prayer exercises suggested in the chapter. How did it make you feel? Is this kind of prayer something you could do on a regular basis?

3. Do you play? If you do, have you ever seen it as an acknowledgement that you are loved unconditionally?
4. If you do not make time for play, what is the real reason?

Chapter 8
Companionship

"Companions are those rare people who ask how we are and then wait to hear the answer."

We all need companionship in our lives. Without some experience of companionship our lives can become lonely and sad. When John Donne said that no man is an island unto himself he was giving expression to the need human beings have to be in relationship. Of course companionship is much more than being social. It is the experience of mutual presence. It is a space where our capacity for life is nourished by others. It creates the possibility of becoming intimate with someone. This is why the type of relationship we call companionship is one of the most beautiful gifts we can give to each other.

There are different models of what companionship actually is. The model that I prefer is one that is found in the scriptures. At the end of St Luke's Gospel (24:13-35) there is a story about the experience of two people as they travelled from Jerusalem to Emmaus after the death of Jesus. The story describes how they were joined on their journey by an apparent stranger who walked with them. Their relationship with the stranger began with the experience of acceptance and ended with a shared meal. On the road there was mutual listening and soulful conversation. In my view this story, known as the Emmaus story, is a deeply rich and meaningful account of the experience of companionship.

Acceptance
In the story companionship begins with mutual acceptance, in fact it begins with mutual unconditional acceptance. Unconditional acceptance is the essential starting point and foundation of companionship. Unconditional acceptance is an attitude that is inclusive and that transcends race, colour, religion, class and sexual orientation. With it there are no conditions and no requirements. There is also no judgement and no condemnation. If there needs to be criticism, this criticism is offered in a way that makes a distinction between the person and the person's behaviour. The renowned psychotherapist, Karl Rogers, discovered in his therapy work that unconditional acceptance or unconditional positive regard as he would put it was absolutely essential if people were to begin a process of healing. When people take off their mask, when they take off the suit of clothes they hide behind they need to know that they are still accepted. Without this type of acceptance there is little or no possibility of companionship developing.

Mutual Listening

A second thing the Emmaus story tells us about companionship is the importance of listening, mutual listening. In the experience of companionship listening, good listening, attentive listening is essential. People need to be heard. To be human is to have a story to tell. We need opportunities to tell our story; we need people to tell our story to. A companion is someone who allows you to tell your story, who encourages you to tell your story, who helps you to tell your story. When we listen, really listen to another we create a welcoming space in our hearts for that person. Often this is enough for the person sharing their story to feel better. A good example of this is to be found in story told by Margaret Wheatley:

"When people tell their stories, they are capable of healing themselves. The act of telling our story, and feeling that we are being listened to, is one of the simplest ways to heal. A young South African woman taught a profound lesson about listening. She was sitting in a circle of women from many nations, and each woman had the chance to tell a story from her life. When her turn came, she began quietly to tell a story of true horror, of how she had found her grandparents slaughtered in their village. Many of the women were westerners, and in the presence of such pain, they instinctively wanted to do something. They wanted to fix it,

to make it better, anything to remove the pain of this tragedy from such a young life. The young woman felt their compassion, but also felt them closing in. She put her hands up, as if to push back their desire to help. She said: 'I don't need you to fix me. I just need you to listen to me.'"(3)

Attentive listening isn't easy. There is always the temptation to interrupt, to respond or react too quickly. We need to learn when it is right to stay quiet and when it is right to speak. If we rush in too quickly with our opinion the other person may close up and an opportunity may be lost. We need to remember that those who have an opportunity to tell their stories to someone who listens attentively find it easier to deal with their circumstances.

Soulful Conversation

On the journey from Jerusalem to Emmaus there was soulful conversation. Soulful conversation is not that common and yet without it there is no real experience of companionship. Soulful conversation is about diving deeper. To have a soulful conversation means that we must be willing to talk about the things we carry in our hearts. In other words we must be willing to talk about what is happening within us emotionally and even spiritually. There is actually a huge need in people to have this kind of conversation. But something prevents it from happening. Perhaps this is fear. We are frightened of revealing our true selves and we are frightened of feeling exposed and vulnerable. The truth is soulful conversation creates emotional and spiritual intimacy and emotional and spiritual intimacy is one of the most enriching and fulfilling experiences we can have. No wonder the two companions walking to Emmaus found themselves saying, "Did not our hearts burn within us as we talked on the road."

Table Fellowship

The word companion comes from two Latin words 'cum' and 'panis' which literally mean 'with bread.' A companion is someone you sit at table with, you break bread with, you share food with. This is sometimes referred to as table fellowship. In the Jewish culture at the time of Jesus the table was a place of acceptance and an invitation to friendship. For the Jews sitting down to a meal was much more than our need for food. It was about relationships; creating relationships and building relationships. Companionship probably happens best over food, around the table. It certainly happens naturally over food, around the table. At the end of their journey to Emmaus the two companions invited the stranger who walked with them to join them for a meal. Significantly it was while they were sitting together around the table that the stranger's true identity was revealed.

We can understand why Jesus used the images of a wedding feast and a great banquet to describe life in the Kingdom of God. The enjoyment of a shared meal accompanied by meaningful conversation and indeed a relaxed silence is a delightful experience.

Jesus

The Emmaus model is of course a gospel model of companionship. It is the kind of companionship that Jesus had with his close group of disciples known as the twelve. Jesus wanted the twelve to experience what companionship is meant to be. He also wants us to experience what companionship is meant to be. This is possible provided we make time for it. It is possible as long as we do not let our fears hold us back, especially our fear of rejection. We can find companions; we are meant to find companions. What is more, we have the offer of the companionship of Jesus.

Speaking of the companionship of Jesus, this is something that is always available to us. Jesus is the invisible companion of our life's journey. He walks the road of life with us. Because of his humanity Jesus knows what it means to be human. This makes him approachable and trustworthy. Jesus is a companion who accepts us unconditionally. He listens attentively to us. He inspires us with his wisdom. And he feeds the hunger in our hearts in the meal of his Eucharist. Jesus longs for our companionship. If we are honest with ourselves we can come to admit that we also long for his.

In a Nutshell

Companionship satisfies the longing within us for a deep connection with at least one other person. The Emmaus Story (Luke 24:13-35) offers us a good model of companionship. This model includes acceptance, mutual listening, soulful conversation and the experience of a shared meal. Because of his humanity, Jesus can also be our companion.

Questions for personal reflection

Once again I suggest that you spend some time with these questions and perhaps do some journaling with them.

1. What do you think of the model of companionship described in this chapter?
2. Remember an experience of companionship you have had. How did it make you feel?
3. Is companionship something you want? What do you need to do to make it happen?

Chapter 9
Compassion

*"Be compassionate as your Father
is compassionate."*
Luke 6:36

Horror gripped the heart of a World War I soldier, as he saw his lifelong friend fall in battle. Caught in a trench with continuous gunfire whizzing over his head, the soldier asked his lieutenant if he could go out into the man's land between the trenches to bring his fallen comrade back. "You can go," said the Lieutenant, "but I don't think it will be worth it. Your friend is probably dead and you may throw your life away." The Lieutenant's words didn't matter, and the soldier went anyway. Miraculously, he managed to reach his friend, hoisted him onto his shoulder and brought him back to their company's trench. As the two of them tumbled in together to the bottom of the trench, the officer checked the wounded soldier, then looked kindly at his friend. "I told you it wouldn't be worth it," he said. "Your friend is dead and you are mortally wounded." "It was worth it? Sir," said the soldier. "What do you mean by worth it?" responded the Lieutenant. "Your friend is dead." "Yes Sir," the private answered, " but it was worth it because when I got to him, he was still alive and I had the satisfaction of hearing him say...."Jim... I knew you'd come."

This is a true story and a moving story. It is a story about friendship. It is also a story about the nature of compassion. Compassion is more than doing deeds of kindness for people who are in need. It is more than fixing things. It is more than finding solutions for people who have problems. In essence compassion is simply about being there for people without pulling back in fear or anger.

Some Descriptions

Compassion is being with others. It is walking with and along-side other people. In a rescue situation it is the difference between throwing a rope into a well and going down into the well. Throwing the rope is a detached action that costs little. Going down into the well is personal involvement in the situation. This is what Jesus did. He chose to become personally involved in our lives. We call this the Incarnation. It is reflected in the name Emmanuel, God with us, which is one of the titles given to Jesus. Indeed Jesus himself in his hour of trial and struggle asked the very same from his companions. "Watch and pray." What I need from you at this time is to stay with me, to be with me.

Compassion can also be described as standing in another's shoes. To stand in another person's shoes is to see the world as they see it, from their perspective. This may not be easy. It may require us to let go of our opinions, our prejudices, our need to be in control. Compassion invites us to allow others to find their own solutions to their problems. This means that we may have to let go of our need to fix things. True dialogue requires this kind of compassion. Openness and a willingness to stand in the shoes of others create the possibility of compromise and consensus.

In its purest form compassion is the ability to feel with others. The word itself literally means 'with passion.' To enter into the passion of others is to be truly compassionate. There is a story told about the French diocesan priest known as the Cure d'Ars. When the only son of an elderly widow died the Cure came to visit her. People expected him to help her make sense of her loss. Instead he simply sat beside her, put his hand on her shoulder and let his tears flow with hers. This is a beautiful example of compassion. Compassion is more than sympathy. It is empathy.

Some Reasons
So why do I believe that compassion is so important. Why do I include it in my three C's? One obvious reason is because it is what the life and ministry of Jesus was essentially about. Jesus put flesh on the Father's compassion for his people. He was the compassionate face of the Father. In fact some would say that compassion sums

up the whole Gospel. It is hard to find a better way of describing what Jesus asks of us than his invitation, "Be compassionate as your Father is compassionate" (Luke 6:36).

Another reason I believe compassion is important has to do with the weakness and fragility of the human condition. Many years ago the then Archbishop of Canterbury, Michael Runcie, wrote an article in a Sunday newspaper in response to a media 'witch hunt.' He was addressing the way the newspapers were attacking a priest in the Anglican Church about an aspect of his moral life and behaviour. Inviting them to have some compassion he said, "In this earthly tabernacle there are many mansions and they are all made of glass." Beautifully put! We are all (including journalists) wounded, weak, vulnerable. We could all display a label, 'Fragile, handle with care.' We could all say with W.B. Yeats, "Tread softly or you will tread on my dreams." The truth is we all need compassion.

A third reason for my focus on compassion has to do with the need to create and build inclusive community. There is a tendency in human nature to divide and to exclude. It makes us feel safe to divide the world into who is right and who is wrong; who is good and who is bad; who is in and who is out; who is worthy and who is unworthy. History has proven this time and time again with devastating consequences. West verses

East; democracy verses communism; Catholics verses Protestants; Islam verses Christianity; liberals verses conservatives; the list could go on! Dividing the world in this way justifies our need to dominate; to be in control; to feel better and more important than others. It often gets politicians and heads of state elected! Yet the reality is no one person or group has a monopoly on the truth and on goodness. Every individual and every group are right and wrong, good and bad, worthy and unworthy. Jesus once told a parable about wheat and weeds growing together in the same field. His followers wanted to act immediately to separate them. But Jesus said no. If you do this you may pull up the wheat with the weeds. Leave both grow together until the harvest. Then it will be easier to separate what is to be kept and what needs to be thrown away.

Compassion does not see people and situations in black and white. It accepts that there are many shades of grey. It is not threatened by difference; in fact it is comfortable with difference. Compassion recognises that every human person is a child of God and that the Father "causes his sun to rise on the evil and the good, and sends rain on the just and the unjust" (Matt 5:45). In answer to the question, "Who is my neighbour?" it responds, "Everyone!" Compassion seeks to include rather than exclude. It breaks down barriers, builds trust between people and creates inclusive community.

For this reason compassion is absolutely essential if there is to be peace among the peoples and nations of the world.

Some Requirements

How then do we become compassionate? How do we develop a compassionate heart? One thing we need to do is accept the Father's compassion. Jesus said, "Be compassionate as your Father is compassionate" (Luke 6:36). The Father looks on us with compassion. The Father treats us with compassion. We must allow the Father be compassionate towards us. If we do, this will help us be compassionate with ourselves. It is a fact that many people find it difficult to offer themselves compassion. Once again this is probably because of low self esteem. We feel we are not worthy of compassion. If we are not able to be compassionate with ourselves it is likely that we will find it difficult to offer compassion to others.

Another thing that helps us to become compassionate is the acceptance of our woundedness and our weakness. One of the most painful journeys we have to make in life is the journey to self acceptance. To really accept ourselves as we are we need to accept our wounds, our weaknesses and our vulnerability. We do not need to be perfect; it is alright to fail. Imperfection and failure are part of the human condition. There is nothing wrong with showing weakness and with being vulnerable. We do not need to protect ourselves behind a coat of armour. Wearing a coat of armour does not allow anyone in, not even God. In saying 'yes' to his humanity Jesus said 'yes' to weakness, limitation and vulnerability. "For we do not have a high priest who is unable to empathize with our weaknesses, but we have one who has been tempted in every way, just as we are" (Hebrews 4:15). We are no different to Jesus. We cannot say 'yes' to our humanity unless we say 'yes' to weakness, limitation and vulnerability. Without this 'yes' it will be very difficult to grow in compassion.

All Mystics

The mystical way is the way of compassion. Down through the centuries mystics testify to this truth. In the Middle Ages, Meister Eckhart insisted that the entire goal of the spiritual life is compassion. "If you were in an ecstasy as deep as that of St. Paul and there was a sick man who needed a cup of soup, it were better for you that you returned from the ecstasy and brought the cup of soup for love's sake." For the sixteenth century Spanish Carmelite reformer, Teresa of Avila, prayer and compassion were like twin sisters; you cannot have one without the other. And closer to our own time we have the experience of Thomas Merton. In his book, *Conjectures of a Guilty Bystander*, he describes a mystical insight he had into the oneness of humanity. Looking at a bustling crowd in the centre of Louisville's shopping district, he realizes that the mystery of God is surrounding us at all times. "I was suddenly overwhelmed with the realization that I loved all those people; that they were mine and I theirs, that we could not be alien to one another even though we were total strangers..... There is no way of telling people that they are all walking around shining like the sun." *(4)* For Merton compassion meant seeing people of all faiths and non as children of the one God and our brothers and sisters. It is significant that he was attending a conference on inter-faith dialogue in Bangkok when he died.

In a Nutshell

Compassion is a reflection of God. It is a way of 'being with' people, especially those who are struggling and suffering. It recognises the weakness and fragility of the human condition. Compassion also helps to build a more tolerant and peaceful world. To become compassionate we first need to be compassionate with ourselves.

Questions for personal reflection

Once again I suggest that you spend some time with these questions and perhaps do some journaling with them.

1. Which of the examples of compassion offered do you like the best? Why?
2. Do you find it difficult to be compassionate with yourself? If so, why?
3. Is living in a tolerant and inclusive society important to you? What role does compassion have in helping to build this type of society?
4. What do you need to do to develop a compassionate heart?

Part 3
The Two Halves of Life

"One cannot live the afternoon of life according to the program of life's morning; for what was great in the morning will be of little importance in the evening, and what in the morning was true will at evening have become a lie."
Carl Jung

Chapter 10
The First Half of Life

"Whoever we think we are, we are not."
Thomas Keating

In recent years the journey of life has been described in terms of two halves: the first half of life and the second half of life with a mid life transition in between. It seems to me that there is a lot of wisdom in this approach. I particularly like it because the two ways I have been describing can in fact be associated with the two halves of life. The first half of life tends to be built around the three A's while the second half of life is an invitation to live according to the values of the three concentric circles.

In his excellent book, '*Falling Upward*' Richard Rohr says that there are three questions we all need to answer in the first half of life. These are: What makes me significant? How will I support myself? Who will go with me? *(5)* As we seek to establish ourselves in the world and create a life for ourselves these are certainly the questions that we must deal with. They are practical questions requiring practical answers. But they also address the emotional needs we have in the first half of life.

Significance

In the first half of life the false self sometimes referred to as the ego takes centre stage. Because of this we look for something that will make us feel significant. We can get our significance from a number of things. One of course is our role and our job. A role provides us with a place in the world. It is a way of defining ourselves. I am a teacher; I am a banker; I am a nurse; I am a mechanic; I am a mother; I am a soldier; I am a minister. Our role tends to be the way we like to describe ourselves. It is also the thing that distinguishes us from others. Without some kind of role we are unlikely to feel significant which can have an effect on our self image and our self esteem.

Another thing that may make us feel significant is wealth. Some people want to become rich because they believe it will make them feel important. It will certainly make them look important in the eyes of the world. The idea of becoming 'a self made man,' is attractive to many people. Wealth and success are status symbols. Money gives us the power to accumulate and the more possessions we have the more significant we will look and feel.

Of course fame is also about significance. If I am famous, people will recognise me; they will look up to me; they will see me as someone special. In recent times we have had a growing number of television talent shows. I wonder what is it the countless numbers of young people who audition for these shows are really looking for. Can it be that they are searching for something that will change the way they feel about themselves? Can it be that they are looking for something to make them feel significant?

The thing or things that make us feel significant in the first half of life are going to be things outside ourselves. A role, wealth, fame are all external things. Sooner or later these things will leave us dissatisfied and perhaps even burned out. Success in our career, endless possessions and hordes of adoring fans can never change the way we feel about ourselves. External sources of significance need to be replaced by an internal source of value.

Finance

The question of finance is obviously an important one not just in the first half of life but throughout our lives. In the first half of life we need to find a way to support ourselves. Usually this is through work which has to do with our role. It is necessary that we have a degree of financial security. If we do not we may become too focused on merely surviving which may prevent us from fulfilling other first half of life tasks.

Of course supporting ourselves and indulging ourselves are two very different things. In the first half of life we can easily fall into the trap of overly indulging ourselves. Treating ourselves to a good time and plenty of everything can have unfortunate and lasting consequences both for ourselves and for others. Good, prudent financial management is something we need to learn in the first half of life.

Belonging

In the first half of life we also need to find people who will go with us. This is about our need to belong. We need to belong to a family. We also need to belong to a community or to a group. In Maslow's hierarchy of human needs belonging is on the third rung. Belonging is about identity. We have our own name, our own history, our own ways of doing things, our own rules. Belonging also makes us feel safe and secure; another of Maslow's essential human needs. Because of this, belonging in the first half of life tends to be inward looking. Its focus is on what defines the family or group we belong to and on the ways our family or group are different from other families or groups. For example, some Roman Catholics define themselves by their opposition to abortion. Their opposition to abortion makes them different and perhaps 'better' than those who agree with abortion. Unfortunately the way we belong in the first half of life can create an exclusive mentality and a critical and judgemental attitude towards those who do not share the same values or faith or lifestyle. It may even lead to attitudes like, 'we are right and you are wrong; we are good and you are bad; we have the truth and you do not.'

The false self will use whatever it can to make us believe that we are better or more important than others. It cannot stand being in second place. It prevents us from becoming compassionate. This is a danger in the first half of life.

It is obvious that the first half of life is an important time in our lives. Hopefully we are able to find our answers to the first half of life questions and to do the first half of life tasks well. But we cannot stay in the first half of life doing first half of life things. We cannot keep feeding the ego and the false self. At a certain point in our lives, when we are ready, the power which the false self has over us needs to be broken. The false self needs to be 'outed.' It also needs to be tamed. This is what the mid life transition is about. To this I will now turn.

In a Nutshell

In the first half of life we need to answer three questions. What makes me significant? How will I support myself? Who will go with me? In the first half of life we are powerfully influenced by the false self and the three A's.

Questions for personal reflection

Once again I suggest that you spend some time with these questions and perhaps do some journaling with them.

1. How have you answered the three first half of life questions put forward by Richard Rohr?
2. What has been your experience of the first half of life?
3. If you have moved into the second half of life are you still doing first half of life things? Why?

Chapter 11
Mid Life Transitions

"In the middle of our life's road
I found myself in a dark wood –
the straight way ahead lost."
Dante

We are familiar with the expression mid life crisis. Another way, perhaps less frightening, of describing this experience is mid life transition. The mid life transition is in fact an invitation to move from first half of life concerns to second half of life values, or to put it another way, to let go of the false self and find the true self. The false self may serve us in the first half of life, but it will not serve us in the second half of life. Sooner or later the true self needs to come out of hiding. It needs to take centre stage. It can no longer allow the false self to suffocate it. This is the work of the mid life transition: to let go of the control the false self has over us and instead to live out of the true self.

The Experience

The mid life transition happens to us. We do not choose it. There is usually a catalyst. This can be failure, disappointment, bereavement, dissatisfaction, loss of job or role, the experience of rejection. The mid life transition is inviting us to let go of the familiar, of what we are used to, of what has been driving us, of what has been defining us. The false self does not give up without a fight, even a battle. It will try everything and anything to survive. This is understandable since it has been operating in us from childhood and since then has been our default way of living and behaving. This is why the mid life transition often leaves us struggling, confused, insecure, anxious, even depressed.

There are many descriptions of the mid life transition and the way it affects people. Here are two; one the experience of a woman in her mid forties; the other the experience of a man at the age of fifty.

In my mid forties my husband had an affair with a work colleague nearly ten years younger. He never had been unfaithful before. I was devastated. The whole reason for my being was lost, snatched away. My life had been centred entirely on that of my husband's –his job, his home, his children, his ambitions, even his friends. I had existed only as one of a pair. I had been the wife of a highly successful and popular executive and the mother of two. Now I felt that I was no one, only a reflection of others. I was totally lost and confused. I was also hurting deeply and felt very angry with my husband. Even though he ended his affair in its early stage and tried to heal the wounds, our relationship was no longer a source of any comfort or consolation. I felt that no one was with me; no one can keep me safe. I drifted into depression. Eventually I sought help through therapy. In time the counselling enabled me to work through the emotions I was feeling. It also helped me realise and accept how emotionally dependent I had been on my husband and how I had been defining myself by my role as a wife and a mother. Gradually I began to find myself and to see myself as an independent person. As time went by I felt a self confidence I never thought was possible.

By the age of fifty I had become the executive of a large company. I was enjoying all the rewards of working hard in a successful business. I had a large house in a wealthy suburb and two luxury cars. I went on three annual holidays. I also belonged to a prestigious golf club where I spent most of my time when I was not in the office. Suddenly one day I found myself asking, "Is this all there is? Are the long hours I spend driving the business the really worth it? Perhaps there is something more?" Yes, at some level within myself I had asked these questions before, but this time it was different. This time I could not ignore them. This time for some reason which I still do not fully understand, I had to take them seriously. And I did. As a result I found myself accepting that it would be better to spend more quality time with my wife and my three teenage children. But I knew that prioritising the significant relationships in my life was not going to be easy. Achievement and success had been important to me. In my life up to now I had been getting my value from my work and my career. I made a decision in favour of a new lifestyle, but letting go of my previous lifestyle was a huge struggle. Now I know I did the right thing.

These are good examples of what can happen to us in mid life. In one case the catalyst for the turmoil was external; it was brought on by the unexpected experience of marital infidelity and betrayal. In the other case the catalyst was something profound that was happening within the person even though he found it difficult to articulate what this was; there was certainly an experience of dissatisfaction about the way he was living his life and a desire for something more.

The mid life transition can happen any time from our late thirties. It can even happen in our sixties. Different people are ready at different times in their lives. The important thing is that when it happens we enter into the process it is inviting. The worst thing we can do is to deny it. Denial will only keep us in the bondage of the false self, familiar and comforting that this may feel. The saying, "there is no gain without pain," is certainly true of the mid life transition.

Support

We cannot manage our mid life transition on our own. We need help. In particular we need to find someone to talk to. This can be a counsellor or a spiritual guide; someone who knows what is happening to us and who can listen with understanding and compassion. Many people will say that it is difficult to find the right person to talk to. I can understand where they are coming from. But perhaps we need to be willing to take a risk. There is the old adage, "When the disciple is ready the master will appear." This carries some wisdom and can be trusted.

In my own life I was fortunate to find good counsellors and guides who helped me through my mid life transition. I needed their support, their attentive listening and their insight. I also needed their encouragement not to be afraid. A wise spiritual director once said to me, "The devil has no power but fear." How true! Fear is powerful and subtle and it is constantly trying to pull us back into the darkness and into old patterns of behaviour. Fear wants to keep us living in the A triangle.

Another thing which can be very helpful during the mid life transition is journaling. Our journal can be like a good friend, even a best friend. In

'The Dry Salvages,' T.S. Eliot writes: "We had the experience but missed the meaning." Journaling helps us to find meaning in our experiences. When we are experiencing a mid life transition it is important that we reflect on what is happening in us and to us. It is said that if we can name our enemy we are half way to defeating him. Personal writing allows us to name our struggle, our confusion, our painful and uncomfortable feelings in a way that is confidential and honest. Only I need to know what I write in my journal. Indeed our journal needs to be strictly private.

Journal writing is about letting the thoughts and feelings flow. It is not about grammatical correctness. If we sit down to put an entry into our journal we must not worry about dotting the i's and crossing the t's. This kind of accurateness only blocks freedom of expression. We are not writing for publication or for examination. Self expression, not perfection is what journaling is about.

The D Process

In my experience there are three questions that are likely to arise in sessions with a counsellor or a spiritual guide if we are going through a mid life transition. One, the first, has to do with **Dissatisfaction.** In mid life there will probably be some experience of dissatisfaction. We have become dissatisfied with ourselves and with our lives in some significant way. Once we admit that we are dissatisfied with our lives we then need to explore what it is that is causing our dissatisfaction? Naming our dissatisfaction in a way that is honest and authentic may not be easy. It will probably take some time. What can be even more difficult is accepting the real causes of our dissatisfaction. Staying involved in the process is important. The outcome will be helpful even liberating. The truth does set us free.

A second question has to do with **Desire**. What is it we long for at this time in our lives? Here again naming our longing or longings is going to take time. Accessing our deepest desires is often a slow and complicated business, one that is greatly helped by an astute guide. I am no longer surprised by the fact that even people on a six or eight day silent retreat struggle to name their deepest desires. What they say they desire at the beginning of the retreat is not what they desire at the end. We must not be afraid to dive deeper and deeper. When Jesus invited Peter to go out into deep waters and put down his nets for a catch he was surely referring to more than fish. He was inviting Peter to look into the depths of his own heart in order to discover what it was he really wanted. We know from the gospels that it took Peter sometime to name and accept his deepest desires.

The third question is about **Decision**. Now that we have been able to name our dissatisfaction and our desires we need to decide what we are going to do or at least what is possible for us to do. Practical action is required if our lives are to change in some way. In his wonderful book '*Second Journey*' Gerald O'Collins says that there are two outcomes to the mid life transition. Drawing on Greek mythology he refers to these as an aeneid and an odyssey. One outcome, an aeneid, is when we decide to do something completely different and our lives take a whole new direction. Like Aeneas we move to another place. The other, an odyssey, is when we decide to return to our previous commitments but live our lives in a new way, with a new set of priorities. With Ulysses we go back home.*(6)* Whichever one we choose only practical, concrete decisions will make it happen.

Gospel Story

A good image for the mid life transition is a gospel story. It is the dramatic account of Simon Peter jumping out of a storm tossed boat into a turbulent sea (Matt 14:22-33). Peter decided to leave the familiarity, safety and security of the boat in response to the invitation of Jesus to come to him across the water. It was a brave move; he was nearly swallowed up by the waves and pulled into the deep, dark abyss. In his powerlessness Peter took hold of the hand of Jesus who saved him from drowning and who 'pulled' him into a deeper level of trust and surrender. Peter experienced the presence and power of Jesus in a way he hadn't known before. When he got back into the boat he was a much freer man.

The mid life transition invites us to step out of the boat. If we have the courage to do so the waters may be turbulent for a time but eventually the power that the false self has over us will be broken and we will be ready to move into the freedom of the second half of life.

In a Nutshell

The mid life transition happens to us. It exposes the way the false self and the A triangle have been at work in our lives. It is a confusing and emotionally painful time. In the mid life transition we need the support of someone who will help us find the answers to these questions: Why am I dissatisfied? What do I truly desire? What do I need to do?

Questions for personal reflection

Once again I suggest that you spend some time with these questions and perhaps do some journaling with them.

1. How do you react to the mid life transition process described in this chapter?
2. Does the thought of a mid life transition frighten you? If so, why?

3. In a mid life transition what is the thing that would help you most?
4. If you have already experienced a mid life transition what was it like for you?

Chapter 12
The Second Half of Life

"We are given a span of years to discover our soul, to choose it, and to live our own destiny to the full."
Richard Rohr

Before I offer thoughts on the second half of life I think it is important to acknowledge the reality. Some people never leave the first half of life. They just cannot let go of their first half of life attachments and addictions. Even though life itself offers these people opportunities to enter the mid life process they do everything they can to resist it. They are too invested in a first half of life identity and lifestyle. Then there are those who take a long time to make it into the second half of life. For these people it happens well beyond mid life, in their fifties or even their sixties. They are not ready any sooner to engage in the process of change and growth that is required. Of course there are some people who actually move into the second half of life at a relatively young age. This can be due to an illness or a disability that makes them acutely aware of what is important and what is not. It can also happen to those who are dying. The following story, told by Thomas Keating, is a very moving example of this:

A young man with AIDS was dying in a hospital, and he was literally shaking from the fear of death. What had been communicated to him as a child was an emotionally charged idea of God as a stern judge ready to bring down the verdict of guilty, or a harsh policeman ever on the watch – someone you would want to avoid meeting. The young man was afraid of dying and going to meet this hazardous God whom he had heard about in early childhood.

One of the nurses came into his room and he asked her, "Can you do something to help me?" She said, "I can give you a treatment called therapeutic touch." He replied, "Please do." The nurse began the gentle treatment. At one point his eyes rolled back and the nurse thought he was going to die, but she kept on with the treatment. When she finished the young man opened his eyes and said, "You'll never know what you just did for me. I have experienced unconditional love." About an hour later, he died. (7)

When we experience ourselves as unconditional love we have moved into the second half of life. If not, we have more work to do because unconditional love is who we really are.

Different Questions
In the second half of life we need to answer a different set of questions than we did in the first

half of life. If there are three questions we are required to answer in the first half of life perhaps there are also three in the second half of life. I am convinced that there are. I would like to suggest that these three questions can be framed as follows: Where does my value really come from? With whom can I experience companionship? What can I do for my neighbour? I invite you to carefully consider whether these questions reflect your own experience, especially if you are in the second half of life. I also invite you to be open to the fact that an answer to each of these questions can be found in the gospels, in the experience and teaching of Jesus.

Within

I mentioned earlier that sooner or later we need to move from external sources of significance to an internal source of value. In the first half of life we find our significance in things outside ourselves, in accumulation, in achievement, in approval. In the second half of life we stop doing this because it no longer works for us. Now we are no longer concerned about what we are. Instead our concern is to discover who we are. The second half of life is the time to find our value within. This means that the second half of life is the time to claim our core truth which put simply is our belovedness. Our belovedness is our original blessing. We were born children of God and children of God we will always be. Our deepest truth is that we belong to God and that God is pleased with us. This means that we do not need to do anything or be someone to earn love. It means that we are loved and lovable as we are. To know who we are in God is to find our value within. It is to be able to say, "I am unconditional love." It is to discover our true selves.

In the second half of life we are no longer emotionally dependent on accumulation, achievement and approval. It is not that we do not need to shop, achieve and be affirmed. It is just that now they do not have the same power over us. We are no longer controlled by them. At some level within ourselves we have 'let go.' Because of this we experience an inner freedom. We are also less restless and more at peace with ourselves and with the world. Perhaps the thing we notice most about the change that happens in us in the second half of life has to do with acceptance. We are now able to accept ourselves as we are.

Of course for all this to happen in the second half of life we need to have an experience of unconditional love. Furthermore we need to find a way of staying in touch with this love on a regular basis. This is why I believe that contemplation can be a great benefit to those in second half of life. As I have already mentioned contemplation is an experience of prayer. It is a way of praying that allows us to let ourselves be loved as we are by

God. Contemplation helps us to accept the gift that has already been given to us, the gift of our belovedness. If we are willing to make some time for contemplative practice in the second half of life there is a good chance that the good work we did in our mid life transition will bear fruit and that we will not be pulled back into the first half of life agenda again. Contemplation provides us with the answer to the great second half of life question: Who are we?

Finding Companionship
There is no doubting the fact that in the second half of life we become much more aware of our need for companionship. We want someone to share our life with, someone with whom we can be emotionally intimate and perhaps even spiritually intimate. This was confirmed in a recent survey on retirement carried out by a national newspaper in England. The top three things that people wanted to have as they got older were health, financial security and a companion. In the second half of life we realise that relationships are more important than work, companionship more fulfilling than achievement.

In practice finding the right person or people with whom we can experience companionship may not be easy. What can make things even more difficult is the fact that the person or persons we chose to go with us in the first half of life may not be interested in real companionship. For example what do we do if our marriage partner is still driven by first half of life preoccupations and has no desire for intimacy? Similarly, what do we do if we are living in a religious community and we are not experiencing the companionship we long for? In these situations some look elsewhere for the intimacy they need. This can take a lot of courage and involve much sacrifice. None of us has a right to criticise or condemn those who choose this course of action.

It must be said that generally women find companionship easier than men. They are more natural at it and because of this they tend to be better at it. Women may prefer to use the word intimacy rather than companionship. In fact, one of the reasons why I am using the word companionship rather than intimacy is because I believe men are less threatened by it. Most men do not find it easy to talk about what is going on within them. They certainly have a tendency to go into their cave to sort things out. Women on the other hand like to talk about their feelings; their instinct is to find someone to share their feelings with. The truth is even though men may find it difficult to be vulnerable and are slow to talk they do have the same need for companionship and intimacy as women. In the second half of life this need seeks fulfilment.

Other People

The late actress, Audrey Hepburn, once said, "As you grow older you will discover that you have two hands, one for helping yourself, the other for helping others." Our lives are not just about ourselves and our own needs. Our lives are also for others. This is something that we become much more aware of in the second half of life. In the second half of life we want to do something that will benefit other people, especially people who are struggling and suffering. I have noticed in the work of spiritual accompaniment that those who are finding their way through a mid life transition often ask themselves the question, 'What can I do to help other people?' Helping other people can take many forms. It can be and often is something very practical like fund raising or working in a charity shop or visiting the elderly or the sick or bringing food to the homeless. But it can also involve making a major decision like going abroad to assist with a humanitarian crisis. It is significant that the twelfth and final step in the Alcoholics Anonymous programme is about giving your life away to others. Until and unless we give our lives away to others we do not seem to have it ourselves at any deep level.

A sign that we have moved into the second half of life is that we are not discriminating about the people we help. This is because our attitude to others is much more accepting and inclusive. We are more interested in what we have in common with other people than in what divides us. It does not bother us whether our neighbours are black, white, Moslem, Christian, Catholic, Protestant, gay, or straight. What is more, we also realise that this world belongs to everyone and that everyone deserves some quality of life. In response to the question, "Who is my neighbour?" Jesus told the story of the Good Samaritan. This is a story about compassionate involvement in life of someone who has a different culture and religion. It is a story that inspires and guides those in the second half of life because those in the second half of life do not put conditions on their compassion.

Already religious pluralism is penetrating all cultures. How we live together with different points of view is becoming more and more important. It is not possible to create this kind of communion without compassion. Compassion offers understanding and respect to everyone in the human family, especially members of other religions. The project of making peace at whatever level requires us to be compassionate. Because of this, compassion is an essential quality in all leaders of state and religion. The best leaders may be those who have the wisdom and disposition of the second half of life.

Home

Needless to say the second half of life is a more peaceful time in our lives than the first half of life. We are no longer restless and given to frenetic activity. We are contented with who we are and with what we have. In the second half of life we have come home to ourselves and to our own hearts. This is the time when we really know what Julian of Norwich meant when she wrote, "all shall be well, and all shall be well, and all manner of thing shall be well."

> **In a Nutshell**
> We move into the second half of life only when we are ready. In the second half of life we answer a different set of questions. These are: Where does my value really come from? With whom can I find companionship? What can I do for my neighbour? The second half of life is built around contemplation, companionship and compassion. It is the time when we come home to our true selves.

Questions for personal reflection

Once again I suggest that you spend some time with these questions and perhaps do some journaling with them.

1. What do you think of the three second half of life questions put forward in this chapter?

2. Does the description of the second half of life appeal to you? Is it something you could look forward to?
3. If you feel you are being invited into the second half of life what do you need to do to get there?

An Overview of the Journey

The Three A's

Accumulation

Approval

Achievement

- First half of life preoccupations and addictions

- Built around external sources of value; we look for happiness in things outside us

- Feeds the false self

The Three D's

Dissatisfaction

Desire

Decision

- Mid life transition process

- Growth in self knowledge and self acceptance

- Movement from the false self to the true self

The Three C's

Compassion

Companionship

Contemplation

- Second half of life values

- Built around an internal source of value; happiness is found inside

- Feeds the true self

Appendix
For Those in
Religious Life

"I will allure her. I will lead her out to the wilderness, and I will speak to her heart."
Hosea 2:14

I would like to conclude with a few thoughts for those in religious life. As I mentioned in the introduction, I was a religious for over thirty years. Indeed from the age of twelve I attended a boarding school run by a religious congregation. Being a member of a religious congregation provided me with security and belonging. It gave me an identity. It also of course made me feel significant. Needless to say my decision to leave religious life around the age of fifty was a huge struggle. My emotional dependency on the congregation was very deep. Probably the thing that helped me most to find a new source of value and security was spending time in silent prayer. Over a period of time I found in my relationship God what I sought from the institution.

In seems to me that for some time now there has been a major struggle taking place within religious life. This struggle is happening both at an institutional level and a personal level and it is creating inner conflict for individual religious. The struggle I am referring to is a struggle between two different lifestyles. I am going to call these lifestyles the monastic lifestyle and the contemplative lifestyle. In making this distinction I am not suggesting that those who live in monasteries are not contemplatives. Monastic life in fact is meant to create a contemplative rhythm and disposition.

Different Lifestyles

The monastic lifestyle tends to be highly structured. It demands fidelity to community life expressed in attendance at community acts. It usually has some form of in house or on site ministry. The monastic lifestyle emphasises external supports, regularity and uniformity. It tends to feed first half of life concerns, especially institutional security, belonging, identity and significance. The monastic lifestyle is built around *observance*. Because of this it can lead to loneliness and emptiness.

The contemplative lifestyle is flexible and fluid. It requires fidelity to spiritual practice especially silent prayer. It encourages and nurtures the experience of companionship. It provides an itinerant ministry. The contemplative lifestyle emphasises internal conviction, unity and trust. It is the way those who have worked through the mid life transition prefer to live. It satisfies our need for intimacy, authenticity and freedom of expression. It is motivated by compassion. The contemplative lifestyle is built around *relationships*. Unfortunately it can create fragmentation and confusion.

As I see things, a number of religious congregations, especially female congregations, have genuinely tried to move from the monastic lifestyle which in many cases was imposed on them by the Church to the contemplative lifestyle. For a number of reasons this has not been easy. Many of the candidates interested in religious life in recent times seem to want a more monastic lifestyle. They are attracted by external signs of belonging and identity, by structure, by institutional security and by a way of life that is clearly defined and offers certainty. They want their formators to stay at home to provide the stability, reassurance and routine they need.

Mystical, not Functional

Then there has been the major problem of letting go of the huge emphasis on function. Many religious define themselves by what they do, by their work. They are teachers, nurses, priests, social workers, pastoral assistants. They seem to be no different than the majority of people who get their significance from their role and their work. Indeed like many they too can give priority to their career. It is not uncommon to meet religious who feel lost when their job and their role are gone. They do not know what to do with themselves and their lives can even feel empty and meaningless. Because for reasons of age and dwindling numbers lay people are taking over the work and the responsibilities of religious this is happening more and more.

It seems to me that the loss of function does not have to be a crisis for religious. In fact it is an opportunity to claim something that is at the very core of religious life. The call to religious life is mystical, not functional. People become religious not because it will provide them with a lifestyle that will help them be good teachers or nurses or priests but because Jesus invites them into this way of life. To make the transition to a more contemplative lifestyle religious must stop defining themselves by what they do. Instead they need to claim the mystical dimension of their vocation. The experience of unconditional love has to be the essential justification for their way of life. And this experience needs to show itself in the way they live.

A New Expression

Traditionally the three pillars of religious life have been presented as prayer, community and service. This way of describing religious life is general enough to cover the variety of forms religious life takes and the different ways in which it is lived. I would like to suggest that perhaps a new and fresh way of presenting the three pillars of religious life is what I have been referring to as the three C's: Contemplation, Companionship and Compassion. Having lived as a religious for many years I believe that religious life needs to be about the values of contemplation, companionship and compassion. It needs to be a way of living these values. I also believe that if religious life is to survive in the developed world in the coming years a genuine attempt to give expression to these values will be necessary. Living these values will not only put new energy into religious life. It will also make it once again a prophetic witness to what is really important. From the beginning religious life was counter-cultural, a lifestyle that caught the attention and interest of people of all walks of life. Today in western society we certainly need the witness and challenge of this kind of lifestyle.

If religious life is meant to be a contemplative lifestyle, a lifestyle built around the values of contemplation, companionship and compassion, then it is more a second half of life lifestyle than a first half of life lifestyle. Needless to say this presents a challenge for those congregations receiving candidates in the first half of life who are looking for first half of life things. Candidates entering religious life in the first half of life need good formation. They need to be helped to grow in self awareness and self knowledge. They need robust programmes that integrate both emotional and spiritual development. They also need to be supported and challenged. If religious life is drawing on the power of the gospel then it should be able to help its members to embrace a lifestyle built around contemplative values. Religious life should be able to give witness to the world that there is another way.

Hope

Whether many of the religious congregations living in the developed world will survive remains to be seen. If they are to survive they are going to need a radical transformation built on radical grace. They certainly need a new expression if they are to capture the imagination of our contemporary culture. This is something we learn from history. Antony of the Desert, Benedict, Francis of Assisi, Teresa of Avila, Roger of Taize and others all caught the imagination of their contemporaries with their creative new lifestyles. Some say that the only way the transformation of religious life can happen is by letting the present forms die and by allowing in time new seeds to bring forth new life. In this they refer to these words of Jesus, "No one sews a piece of unshrunken cloth on an old cloak; if he does, the patch pulls away from it, the new from the old, and the tear gets worse. And nobody puts new wine into old wineskins; if he does the wine will burst the skins and the wine is lost and the skins too. No! New wine, fresh skins!" (Mark 2:21-22) Whatever the future, religious life will always exist because God invites people in every generation to live this way of life as a prophetic sign of what is important: contemplation, companionship and compassion.

In a Nutshell

There is a struggle taking place in religious life at both the institutional and personal level. This is a struggle between two different lifestyles; the monastic lifestyle and the contemplative lifestyle. The invitation to live as a religious is mystical, not functional. Religious life needs new forms of expression. These forms of expression need to be built around the gospel values of contemplation, companionship and compassion.

Questions for personal reflection

Once again I suggest that you spend some time with these questions and perhaps do some journaling with them.

1. Do you agree with this assessment of what is happening in religious life in the developed world? How does it correspond with your experience?
2. Do you personally desire a more contemplative lifestyle in the way you are living as a religious?

3. What needs to happen in your congregation if it is to adopt a lifestyle built around the gospel values of contemplation, companionship and compassion?

Another Parable

There was once a poor rabbi who lived in the city of Krakow. He lived on the street of the Lost Angel, in the last hovel on that street with his wife and his four children. Since he was very poor, he dreamed every night of riches. But one night the dream was exceptionally vivid. He dreamed that underneath a bridge in the city of Warsaw there was a treasure. When he awoke in the morning, he excitedly told his wife and his children about his dream. He then packed food and clothes and set off on the long journey to find that bridge. He travelled many long days and nights and finally arrived at Warsaw. It was just as the dream had pictured – except for one thing. There was a guard on the bridge, a sentinel who paced back and forth. And so the poor rabbi, tired from his journey, fell asleep in the bushes. When he awoke, he rattled the bushes with his arm and the guard spied him.

"You there, come here!" He was a simple man and he did not run. He sheepishly came forward. The guard said, "What are you doing here?" The simple man who would not run was a simple man who would not lie. He said, "I have dreamed that underneath this bridge there is a treasure and I have travelled many long miles to find that treasure and be rich." The guard said, "That is strange!

Just last night I too had a dream. I dreamt that in the city of Krakow, on the street of the Lost Angel, in the last hovel on that street, where lives a rabbi and his wife and four children, there is buried behind the fire place a treasure. But, it's just a dream. It can never be true. Now, you, you get out of here before I run you in. Never let me see you again!"

So the rabbi raced away and took the long journey back home. He went to his house on the street of the Lost Angel, went into his parlour, moved away the fireplace, dug underneath and found the treasure and lived happily ever after.

Notes

1. Marcus J. Borg, *The Heart of Christianity* (HarperOne 2004), pp. 190-191
2. See Josef Pieper, *In Tune with the World: A Theory of Festivity* (New York: Harcourt, 1965), pp. 35-36.
3. Margaret J. Wheatley, *Speaking our Suffering* (published on her website margaretwheatley. com in 2002)
4. Thomas Merton, *Conjectures of a Guilty Bystander* (Bantam Doubleday Dell, 1994), pp. 140-141
5. See Richard Rohr, *Falling Upward* (Jossey-Bas, 2011), p.1
6. See Gerald O'Collins, *Second Journey* (Gracewing, 2000), pp. 70-71
7. Thomas Keating, *The Human Condition* (Paulist Press, Mahwah, N.J. 1999), pp. 44-45

Reading List

Boulle, Robert. *Going Toward your Truth.* Cambridgeshire: Melrose Books, 2010

Campbell, Antony. *God First Loved Us.* Mahwah N.J.: Paulist Press, 2000

Gallagher, Michael Paul. *Free To Believe.* London: Darton, Longman and Todd Ltd, 1991

Hughes, Gerard W. *God of Surprises.* London: Darton, Longman and Todd Ltd, 1986

Keating, Thomas. *The Human Condition.* Mahwah N.J.: Paulist Press, 1999

Manning, Brennan. *Abba's Child.* Colorado: NavPress, 2002

Manning, Brennan. *A Glimpse of Jesus.* New York: HarperCollins, 2004

Naish, John. *Enough.* London: Hodder & Stoughton, 2009

Nouwen, Henri. *The Return of the Prodigal Son.* London: Darton, Longman and Todd Ltd, 2001

Nouwen, Henri. *Life of the Beloved.* London: Hodder & Stoughton, 1993

Nouwen, Henri. *The Inner Voice of Love.* London: Darton, Longman and Todd Ltd, 2010

O'Collins, Gerald, *Second Journey.* Herefordshire, England: Gracewing, 2000

Robb, Paul. *Passage Through Mid-Life.* Notre Dame Indiana: Ave Maria Press, 2005

Rohr, Richard. *Falling Upward*. San Francisco: Jossey-Bas, 2011

Rohr, Richard. *Immortal Diamond*. London: SPCK Publishing, 2013

Rupp, Joyce, *Dear Heart, Come Home*. New York: The Crossroad Publishing Company, 2006